The Full English

"...engaging, informative, entertaining and very, very witty. This bloke makes good writing look as easy as riding a bike. I wish it was..."
George East, best-selling author of The Mill of the Flea series

"A delightfully tongue in cheek trip through England - past and present. Along the way you'll find out about: Terry - Druid Keeper of the Stones, wartime secrets of the Gurkhas, the Society For The Prevention Of Getting Lost In The English Countryside, and much more."
Richard Peace, cycling journalist an author of the Excellent Books range of cycle guides

"Mike Carden's epic bike ride offers a unique and fascinating view of England, both past and present. Combining historical insight with laugh out loud humour, 'The Full English' is warm, wonderful and unforgettable."
Megan Taylor, author of How We Were Lost, Flame Books

Published by
Bike Ride Books

www.bikeridebooks.co.uk

First published in Great Britain in 2007 by Bike Ride Books

Printed in England

Cover illustration by Robin Grenville-Evans, 2007

ISBN 978-0-9556602-0-7

Bike Ride Books
Rannerdale, 39 Market Place,
Cockermouth, Cumbria, CA13 9DP, Great Britain

THE FULL ENGLISH

Pedalling through England, Mid-Life Crisis
and
Truly Rampant Man-Flu

Mike Carden

Beginning

As I stood on the edge of the low cliffs holding on to the bike, the sea below was surging past the rocks, breaking and foaming. Behind me, the red-and-white striped lighthouse marked the southernmost tip of Dorset in the centre of the south coast of England – Portland Bill.

Wisely, I feel now, I decided that dipping the bike's wheels in the water just here had not been my best idea ever.

The bike.

Was I really going to keep calling it 'the bike' as I zig-zagged from one end of England to the other? Parts of me were going to get to know 'the bike' fairly intimately on a journey to the furthest north point in England at Berwick-upon-Tweed.

Through Glastonbury, Ludlow and the Peak District. Then the Yorkshire Dales, and along the Northumbrian coast to the border.

Twelve counties.

650 miles.

After all that, would 'the bike' still be 'the bike'?

"What do I call you, bike?"

Bike: "Well, the name on the side is PURGATORY."

Me: "That may be very descriptive but I can't see me leaning you outside a chip shop and saying, 'Stay, Purgatory, stay.'"

Bike: "No. I see what you mean."

Me: "Purgy?"

Bike: "Don't even think about it."

Me: "So, any other ideas?"

Bike: "I'm a Scott."

Me: "Ah."

Long pause.

Me: "Stay, Scott, stay." Another pause. "That works." And another. "Sit, Scott, sit."

Bike: "Are you trying to be funny?"

I'd settled for shorts and a bike shirt for the hazy start to the day, with the sea bluer than the sky. Warm clothes, tools and food were in my panniers. I was ready. I checked my watch. Seven minutes past nine on a Sunday morning in May. Sort of ready, anyway. I had never done anything like this before. A long bike ride. Mostly unaccompanied. Well, except for Scott.

It was an odd feeling.

I looked again at the waves breaking on the rocks below. No, I would need a plan B, and I decided that Portland Beach would be it. The beach was at the other end of this little island, just before the causeway to the mainland. That would be better for the old dipping-the-wheels-in-the-water-before-an-epic-bike-ride thing.

So why was I doing this epic ride? This was a question I would ask myself more than once.

It was partly 'the challenge'. All those miles. All those hills. But only partly. There was a second reason.

I wanted to look at England. Not the big towns and cities, so similar from one end of the country to the other. And definitely not the A-roads with their by-passes, roundabouts and dual carriageways. No. I wanted to see the villages, the hills, the farms, the land, and mostly, the history. I wanted to do it at bike speed, stopping off to look around when the fancy took me. I wanted to bike England, the real England.

5

There is a faint possibility that there was a third reason, which I hadn't even mentioned to myself yet, let alone anybody else. There I was, mid-forties, with no sign yet of an urge to buy a fast, red, noisy sports car, but instead setting off on a 650-mile bike ride with a dodgy knee and accompanied by a bike with attitude. Mid-life crisis? What mid-life crisis?

There were two bird-watchers in matching male and female moss-green jackets behind the lighthouse. Standing at the edge of the cliffs, they were scanning across the sea with binoculars fixed on tripods.

"Here they come. Left to right," the man said, talking the birds down, like they had ground-to-air missiles.

I tried to see what they could see, gannets perhaps, streaking across, fast and low. But I could see nothing.

"Coming through now."

"Got them."

I swung on to the saddle and pushed off, leaving behind me the sea and those ground-to-air missiles.

The land started to rise.

"Is there much of this?" Scott said.

"No. Hardly any."

I stopped and looked back. Somewhere out of sight in the distance was France. Somewhere ahead of me was Berwick-upon-Tweed. I couldn't actually see it from the Dorset coast, but nevertheless, that's where it was. North.

I patted his handlebars. "Hardly any at all."

"Good," he said. "Because I don't like hills. Or long distances."

"Ah," I said.

The Route

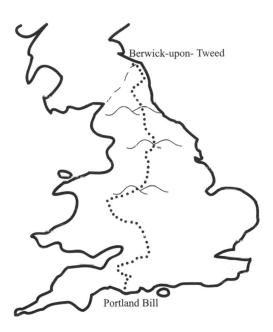

Berwick-upon- Tweed

Portland Bill

Possibly.

Part One

Day One

Target: 42 miles from Portland Bill to Sherborne, via Maiden Castle and Dorchester

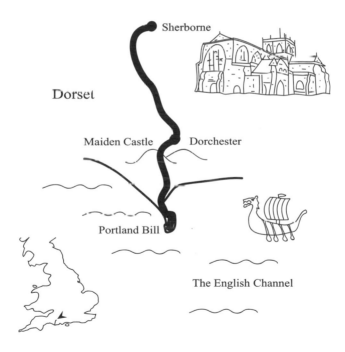

Portland is how the moon will look after it has been colonised for a few years and given air, grass and seawater. Even when all that is done, the moon will still have giant lumps of moon rock carefully placed to prevent space ships parking on a verge, or driving over a cliff into the surging sea below. Portland is short on space ships, long on moon rock.

The view grew as my road climbed gently away from the the bird watchers and the moon-rocked car park. The sea was still blue, but waves were starting to scud as the breeze got up. With only half a mile gone, I pulled over, cold, to put a t-shirt over my bike shirt. Getting cold wouldn't help the sore throat I had brought with me, and going down with a bug wasn't part of the plan.

"Are we nearly there yet?" Scott said.

"Nearly," I said.

Pulling over had also helped my legs and my breathing of course. I suspected that there might be a lot of stopping half-way up hills to look at views or to deal with clothing.

I cycled on towards Easton. Easton as opposed to Weston, on the other side of the island, which has a certain symmetry.

There were more lumps of Portland stone dotted along the route, some of them massive and signalling the presence of giant quarries for the sought-after stone used for St Paul's Cathedral, the British Museum and so many more of England's monuments. The stone is also used for Portland's own buildings, and in the May sunshine Easton took on an almost homely air. In a dark November, those grey buildings might seem quite different.

The road dropped steeply down from the island towns, past a monument to the people of Portland – the stone-cutters and fishermen – and towards the causeway linking the island with the mainland.

Chesil Beach began on the west side, its pebbles stretching for miles along the coast. On the right was Portland Beach and – surprisingly – a Viking longboat had parked on the beach. It must have been on double-yellow lines, because hairy Scandinavian warriors were about to commit the first ever murder of an Anglo-Saxon traffic warden with a double-headed battle-axe.

Actually that's only partially true. It was not 789AD; and the only other figure on the beach at 9.20 on this Sunday morning was a man with a fishing rod.

I pushed Scott down the beach towards the water, tyres scrunching through the pebbles, and nodded at the fisherman.

He had a stool a few metres back from the water. "You'll not get to France on that," he said.

"What?"

"The bike."

"Oh. No, I'm just going to wet the wheels."

He looked at me for a moment. "Does it make them go faster?"

What do you say to that? Here you are about to start a journey from the sea in Dorset right up to the sea at Berwick-upon-Tweed. And a fisherman in a green cagoule wants to know if dipping your wheels in the sea makes the bike go faster.

"Yes," I said.

In 789AD there was no England. Never had been. There were four different Anglo-Saxon kingdoms covering the land that came to be England. But 789AD saw the first Viking raid on these shores. A Norse longboat had appeared, and when a local official went to investigate, they killed him. That raid was at Portland Beach, somewhere near where I leaned Scott against a moon-rock.

It was the first of the raids and then invasions that would destroy three of the four Kingdoms, leaving just Wessex. When the tide turned, and the Anglo-Saxons fought back, they eventually re-took the southern half of the island of Britain. What they created was one Kingdom. Angloland. The England I was cycling across.

The causeway joining Portland to the mainland has a straight, flat road, and I whizzed along. A great bank of golden pebbles stood high on my left, and on the right pink flowers dotted the grass, with the blue of Portland Harbour beyond, and moored sailing boats drifting in the breeze.

I took a sign to the right for a cycleway to lead me towards Weymouth. It turned out to be an old railway line, now tarmac, and popular with dog-walkers and baby-walkers. The route led in and out of trees, always close to the sea. I used my old-fashioned, tring-tring bell several times, and that should immediately tell you that I was not a proper long-distance cyclist, head down, eating up the miles. I felt more like a pedestrian on wheels. Nursing a dodgy foot, an occasionally painful knee and a wonky wrist, I did have some serious doubts as to whether I could really make it 650 miles.

The bike lane ran out, and real roads emerged. I had planned my route to avoid A-roads (and B-roads if I could), but it was not always going to be practical, and the Weymouth by-pass lay ahead of me.

We set off up the straight but rising road, with the weekend's traffic starting to build up. Small England flags fluttered from car windows in a pre-World Cup frenzy of optimism. An optimism that is traditional and which I shared, and yet which I knew was likely to be entirely misplaced.

At the top of the hill I took signs for the main Dorchester road, but then was mighty pleased when I was able to turn off and to glide on to country lanes. Suddenly the sea was gone, and might be miles away. In the village of Upwey there were white-walled cottages with golden thatch and a stream alongside the road with a 'Mind the Ducks' sign. Astonishingly there was also a sign for 'Well Dressing'.

In Derbyshire each summer, it is traditional to 'dress' the wells – an ancient ritual, Christianised in the depths of time. Had it crept down to Dorset?

I pulled in next to the Wishing Well Café. Two ladies

were painting windowsills of the cottage next door.

"Um," I said, "I saw signs for well-dressing."

"Yes. Just walk through the café."

A lady looked at me from the kitchen.

"Well dressing?" I asked.

"Through the back."

Outside was a green oasis of a water-garden. Flowers, grasses, mosses, and as I turned a corner, water was bubbling up through a pool. The source of the river Wey that would flow out at Weymouth. Behind was an alcove seen through two arches. On the back wall were images of classical instruments – cello, piano, harp, French horn and more. I took them to be painted at first and moved closer.

A couple were spraying the images from a water-bottle and I realised that these were not paintings. They were put together from flowers, leaves, nuts, twigs and acorns.

Twenty years ago the couple had moved from Derbyshire, and evidently they had brought the idea of well-dressing with them.

"It's beautiful," I said.

They were delighted, and even more so when I told them that I hoped to cycle through Derbyshire in a week or so and had not thought to find well-dressing on the south coast.

"Say hello to Bakewell for me," the lady said, and she gave me a photograph of the well. I turned it over and found her name on the back. Maggie, I thought, I will send you a postcard from Derbyshire.

From Upwey there was a long, long hill, and the sun had burned off the haze of cloud. My legs became heavier as the road climbed. My speed was next to nothing. I was in the lowest gear there was.

In Portland at twenty past nine it had been cool and windy. I'd put on an extra t-shirt. Now, I was sweltering and sweating, and by the top I needed to stop. This was hard. Whose idea was it anyway?

With the brakes on, to stop Scott rolling backwards, I clumsily got off, and eased him flat to the ground. My legs didn't feel good. I was breathing hard, and sweating rather too copiously. I took off a layer and my bike-shirt felt distinctly clammy. I stowed the spare t-shirt away in one of Scott's panniers.

From the ridge I could see my next destination – Maiden Castle, the largest hill fort in Europe. I set off down the long hill, chilly now as the wind went through my damp shirt.

I'd been told that there was a bridle-way that I could push my bike up to get into the site from the south. I stopped to ask a dog-walker and she confirmed it. How I missed it, I'm not really sure. What I found was a footpath leading straight up the side of the hill. Thinking this must be it, I pushed and pulled Scott up through a field (Scott: "Are you sure about this?" "Yes."), carried him over a stile, and found myself amongst earthworks.

There were a small number of people about as I lugged the bike self-consciously along the top of various earthworks. Dog walkers, families, General Vespasian of the 2nd Legion. Oh no, that was then.

'Then' was 43AD, and the Roman army was busy conquering Iron Age England. Separate British tribes defended themselves using hill forts all across southern England. This hill fort – 'Mai Dun' or Big Hill – was the biggest. It's bigger than 50 football pitches, bigger than the Bluewater Shopping Centre. This was a Big Hill.

The first inhabitants were Stone Age people around 5,000 years ago, users of flint tools. The ramparts where I was standing now were built about 2,500 years ago by more developed tribes – users of iron tools and weapons.

The ramparts are still six metres high, even after centuries of wind and rain. Originally they were topped by wooden walls, with gates set at staggered intervals in the three rings of ditch and bank. It would have been a huge and impressive sight in its glory, and that might have been its purpose. After all, there is no water at the top of these chalk hills, so it seems unlikely that they were lived in permanently. Perhaps they were status symbols.

"My hill fort is bigger than your hill fort."

"Yes, but have you met my friend General Vespasian?"

Did the Celts really make a stand here against General Vespasian? When the site was excavated in the 1930s, a skeleton was found with a Roman spearhead still embedded in its spine, and this was thought to prove that the General had fought his way in here. More recent archaeologists say that the warrior was buried here, but that there is no evidence of a battle here at all. They speculate that the victims of a battle elsewhere might have been brought up here for their funeral rites.

I laid Scott down on a rampart looking over Dorchester. The day was clear now, and the town below looked like a model village. In fact, it was very pleasant sitting in the sun. The only thing was, how was I going to get down? I seemed to have managed to get my bike into a part of the hill fort where bikes were not meant to be. I was on the top of a large bank, with the only way towards the car park defended by a fence, a stile, steep steps down the grassy hill, and then more steps up onto the next ring of earthworks. Presumably the process would be repeated at that point.

My brother Steve phoned on my mobile. Steve is my oldest brother. A keen cyclist, he's used to cycling long distances. Fixing broken chains. In fact, a good man to have with you on a 650-mile bike-ride. Shame he wasn't coming really.

Steve had provided a bed for the night before and a lift to Portland. Then he'd driven to the end of my day's ride, left his car, and cycled back to the mid-point at Dorchester to join me for the afternoon. A good man, Steve.

"I'm here," he said.

"That's fine. I'll be with you soon. Well, as soon as I can

find my way out of Maiden Castle."

A family came towards me, perky father, loyal mother, and bored teenage son. Perky father confirmed that the stile was the only route to the car park. Loyal mother nodded. Bored son ignored me and went on thinking that he could have been on his Playstation.

I examined Scott from a healthy distance. Underneath, he was a mountain bike. Not, I should say, an expensive one, but at least one with 21 gears and a bit of suspension on the front. So a proud mountain bike. To which I had added flat road-tyres, three panniers at the back, another pannier at the front, an interesting concoction of mud-guard and sticky tape, and the bell. I wondered if I had also added a chip on his shoulder.

Under the eyes of two men leaning on the fence, I took the panniers off and hefted them over the stile, then clumsily lifted Scott over. I carried the panniers down the hill, and went back up again. Then awkwardly wheeled Scott down the stepped track, holding the brakes to stop him carrying me into the ditch, fitted the panniers back on and pushed up the steps on the far side to the top of the next rampart.

The two men seemed to find this lengthy process a touch amusing. Why wasn't there a Roman spear to hand when you really needed one?

A path down appeared, heading for the road to Dorchester, to what the Romans did next, and to lunch with Steve. To hell with it, I thought, and rode Scott down, bouncing on divots.

It was a good job the Romans hadn't attacked Maiden Castle on bikes. I could just imagine them thinking, 'to hell with it', bouncing down over the divots, and heading back to Gaul.

"How far did you say you were going today?" Steve said when we had met up in Dorchester.

"42 miles," I said, through cheese sandwich.

He leaned back against our bench and ran his fingers through his straggly trade-mark beard. Although in this litigious age, I guess that should be Straggly Beard™. "The thing is," he said, "I've just cycled back from Sherborne on a straighter road than you're planning, and that was 19 miles. Your route must be at least 25 miles from here."

"Ah."

"How far have you cycled today?"

"22 miles."

"And how far did you expect?"

"17."

"Wasn't this going to be an easier day?"

"Well, yes."

"Not 47 miles?"

Next to me, Scott was growling. I kicked his front tyre.

General Vespasian was probably gone before Dorchester's Roman Town House was built.

Its low walls are tucked away incongruously behind the County Council offices. It took Steve and me some time to find it.

It was not a grand villa with great swathes of cultivated land around, but a relatively modest house within the town walls of Roman 'Durnovaria'. Today, glass walls and a modern tiled roof keep off the weather, yet allow you to see what is left of the complicated mosaics made of small coloured tiles. Knot patterns and animals are now faded, but would have been bright with colour, the designs reflected in wall paintings.

The Romans occupied the southern half of Britain for close to 400 years, plenty of time for the country and the towns to be completely 'romanised'. And here was the evidence. Steve and I poked around, joined by a coach party, peering through the glass, with the sun warm on our backs.

The house had under-floor heating. The stone slab flooring was raised up on pillars so that warm air would flow through, and experiments have apparently shown that just a small fire kept going each day would warm the whole house.

Water was piped in as well. The Romans built a covered pipeline, 2m wide and 3m deep, to bring water down the valley into Durnovaria, roughly along the line of cycle-route 26 which I was hoping to follow.

This was all such an extraordinary jump in technology from the time of Maiden Castle. Like now, progress must have seemed inevitable. History could only advance. Apparently.

As we came out of the grounds, our own progress also seemed inevitable – there was a sign for NCN 26: one of the growing number of National Cycle Network routes around the country. The NCN routes are designed to join towns via country lanes, tracks and occasionally specific cycle-only routes. I had a map which showed the start of the route on B- and A-roads, but in fact the signposts took us on to brand new cycleways. It was wonderful. Flat tarmac paths, new little bridges, and we were out in the countryside.

When this new link ran out, we found ourselves on country lanes, following little blue NCN 26 signposts. The sun was shining. The hedgerows were wide, two hedge-widths wide, and full of bluebells.

At least, I think they were bluebells. I am not widely famed as a plantsman. They were blue though, so I think I am on safe ground. Full of bluebells, those hedgerows.

I felt good – the legs a little tired perhaps, but no sign of the sore throat, and no trouble with the dodgy wrist, foot or knee. All was right with the world. The trouble was, I still had another 25 miles to go, and before we knew it, those keen makers of NCN 26 were taking us on to farm tracks, some of them rutted and gravelled. Most annoying though was the number of farm gates. It got warmer, and progress slowed. The cool of Portland Bill seemed like a different day. This might be a long ride.

The Roman Empire collapsed from the centre, not from its north-western periphery in Britannia. True, there were an increasing number of raids from the Celtic lands and from across the North Sea, but nothing that the romanised people south of Hadrian's Wall couldn't cope with – so long as they were part of the Empire. Inside the Empire, they had organisation, structure, an army, trade, coinage. When, in 410AD, Rome announced that Britannia was on its own, and withdrew soldiers to help fight the barbarians attacking Italy, Britannia began to implode. Not all at once. Perhaps Durnovaria continued as a civilised town for some time. But before long Maiden Castle was being used again.

We were cycling up the valley of the River Frome, which took a low route between the hills of Dorset, many of which have hill forts, originally pre-Roman, but which mostly would have been re-used during those increasingly unstable times.

Within a few generations, Germanic tribes had filtered through from the coasts. These were 'Angles' from southern Denmark, and Saxons from northern Germany. In some areas, such as the Isle of Wight, the Romano-British people were exterminated. In others, they would have been absorbed. Either way, by the 6th century, this land was Saxon: the Kingdom of Wessex.

The Frome valley would have looked very different from what Steve and I were seeing. Instead of gentle hills with fields either side, much of this would have been forest. Old forest, patches of dark and light underneath a summer canopy of oak and ash and beech. Deer, boar and red squirrels. No background noise of cars and planes. No jet-streaks of white cloud in the sky.

Some straight Roman roads would still just about have existed, but more and more the jerky, twisty tracks would have joined up the growing villages throughout the forests. Those tracks would become today's roads, with all their wanton loops and bends, and only in recent years would they be straightened out again as a Roman might have planned them.

The off-road section of NCN 26 came to an end, and Steve and I were back on those wanton loops through preposterously beautiful villages of flint-set walls and thatch.

We stopped for biscuits in Maiden Newton. A portly local said, "That's the way to travel," but I don't think he had been far on a bike for a while.

Maiden Newton, according to the Heart of Wessex Railway website, is 'a village in the heart of the rolling chalklands of Dorset. The Queen spent the night there on the Royal train in the early 1950s.' Now that is some claim to fame. It goes on to say, 'The town has a pleasant, almost French air.' I couldn't actually smell the garlic.

The route took us past Sutton Bingham reservoir, and a lay-by offered an ice-cream van. Steve and I braked as one. There were a good few cars parked, a Sunday afternoon day-out to watch sailing boats trying to find wind.

"Are you going far?" a white-haired man said. There were three other heads of white hair in the car behind him.

"I'm not," Steve said. "He's going to Berwick-upon-Tweed."

"Oh," he said, looking at me. "That's a long way."

It was starting to feel a long way. My legs ached. The bike computer suggested that it might be even further than 47 miles. And the small hills along the route were feeling like big hills.

"Very nearly there," I said to Scott when we set off again.

Steve looked across. "Sorry?"

"Nothing."

By the time we had arrived in Sherborne, the bike computer said 49.89 miles.

Sherborne looked a lovely little town, with an abbey and

old schools. We loaded the bikes on to the back of the car, and strolled up to the abbey. It was founded by the Saxons after their conversion to Christianity, and still has a stone coffin of one of Alfred the Great's older brothers. The current building is much later – medieval – with a glorious ribbed ceiling of stone.

If I wasn't so tired, I'd have spent longer looking around, but the car, and Steve's house, beckoned. Tomorrow and Glastonbury would wait.

Captain's log: Day One
Distance: 49.89 miles / 79.82Km
Average speed: 11.0mph / 17.6Kmph
Maximum speed: 31.4mph / 50.24Kmph
Minimum speed (not including stopping):
                3.2mph / 5.12Kmph
Legs: blooming tired

Day Two

Target: 41 miles from Sherborne to Street, via Somerton and Glastonbury

It was an hour's drive from Steve's house and he had to be at work for 9 o'clock. So he dropped me at 8 and was gone. It was a rainy Monday morning in Sherborne. The sore throat was back, and I now had a runny nose. I wheeled the bike under a tree and plonked my panniers on to a bench to sort them out. Tissues in pocket. Drinks and sandwiches in a rear pannier. Tissues in front pannier. Waterproof top and helmet on. Tissues in rucksack. That, I thought, should be enough tissues for half an hour or so.

Now I just needed my bike computer in place and I could be off.

The uniformed school children from Sherborne's private schools showed only mild interest in the man in a yellow waterproof jacket pulling clothes and tools from panniers in an increasingly desperate attempt to find his bike computer. Before long my world was distributed across a bench. Half an hour later, and very chilly, I gave up. I must have left it at Steve's. Somehow, it felt a real blow. I would have no idea how far the epic ride really was. Perhaps Steve could post it on to me. For today, I would have to guess how my actual mileage compared to my plans.

I stuffed everything back into place and mounted up. The rain wasn't heavy, but it was persistent. 'Persistent', it occurred to me, is a very positive, hopeful word. So why does it get associated with rain? Like 'it's trying to rain'. Why try? Just leave it. Go home and lie down, rain.

I had no idea which way to cycle to get out of town. Signposts are generally designed to lead cars through towns and out the other side. They are not placed to help a cyclist starting at a random point somewhere in a town. I cycled in what felt like a northerly direction, and came across a bike shop. I had hoped for friendly cyclist greetings and full directions, but instead decided to look up the word 'curmudgeonly' in the dictionary when I got home.

When I finally found the road I was looking for, it had a

familiar sign. It was a continuation of NCN26, complete with little blue signs. The road rose gently through a valley, with the hedgerows changing from bluebells to white cow-parsley. Well, probably cow-parsley, but I'm prepared to be contradicted.

Either way, white and green was replacing blue and green. I was approaching Somerset. One county down. Just the eleven to go then.

The road dropped damply down into the village of Marston Magna ("Two pints of Marston Magna and a packet of Cheese and Onion please.") and suddenly levelled out. As I passed the airbase at Yeovilton, the rain stopped. A few more ups and downs, and there was the one of the best town signs I have seen:

Somerton
The Royal Capital of Ancient Wessex

Some signs give too little information. Some too much. Take the sign I had seen on a training ride close to my home in Cumbria. I was passing a tiny village green surrounded by cottages and houses, when I noticed a well at the back, edged by stone flags standing on end. I could make out a sign next to it, so I heaved off the bike and walked across, fully expecting a sign saying that this was an ancient celtic well and that many votive offerings had been found. Or that this was the real source of the Thames. Or that Queen Victoria had come to take the water. Something anyway. Not:

No Dogs
No Kite Flying

Kite flyers? You take my point, anyway. I wanted more information on the Cumbrian sport of kite-flying-while-standing-in-a-well, and the sign was no help at all.

Anyway, the Somerton sign was perfect. No silly little

symbols telling you that there is a library and a swimming pool. No 'Somerton welcomes careful drivers but actively discourages pedestrians and cyclists'. Instead, just enough to whet the appetite: there must surely be great earthworks, maybe complete town walls, perhaps a huge statue of the god, Woden.

The route into town led me past 'Light Bites', and suddenly I was hungry. Very, very hungry. I had cycled for a couple of hours after a quick bit of breakfast and here was a menu that said 'sausage and bacon sandwich' and also 'tea' and 'flapjack'. So that was me for a good half hour.

The centre of Somerton has a church and a market cross, together worth a few minutes perusal, but I was after The Royal Capital of Ancient Wessex. I went in to the Tourist Information Centre to ask. Were there any leaflets or booklets to tell me all about it? To guide me around the ancient capital? The earthworks, the town walls, Woden? No, apparently. Nothing? Well, no. I had been misled. The town sign was wasted. I would cycle on to somewhere more interesting.

The plan now was to take a circuitous route to see the Peat Moors Visitor Centre and Glastonbury, before ending up at the hostel in Street. It wasn't the shortest route by any means, but the rain had gone and the sniffly nose wasn't too bad. All I had to do was find the route.

I took an educated guess for a road that I thought should lead me to High Ham, a little village on a ridge, from where I could cut north. From there it would be absolutely flat, since I would be cycling across the drained peat lands of the Somerset Levels. Easy really.

Unfortunately I had not bargained on the signposting in Somerset. Later, I wrote a Letter of Complaint:

SPOGLITEC
Society for the Prevention Of
Getting Lost In The English Countryside

The Head of Signposts
The Highways Department
Somerset County Council
County Hall
TAUNTON
Somerset
TA1 4DY

Dear Sir (or Madam)
I would like to inform you that Somerset County Council has been unanimously voted by the membership of SPOGLITEC as having the poorest signposting of country roads in southern England. I would specifically point out that the lack of signposts led me to see the village of High Ham, perched on its ridge, twice on my recent cycle ride. Also that Henley seemed not to exist.
I did try my usual Zen direction-finding, but even that failed me. I was almost reduced to getting more in touch with my feminine side by asking for directions, but there was nobody to ask.
Further east, there were numerous turnings off country lanes with no signposts, leading me to go off my planned route and to experiment with the use of certain Anglo-Saxon phraseology whilst conducting a u-turn on my bike. Not easy, I am sure you will agree.
On pointing all this out to a gentleman at Oldford, he said, "Well at least you will have no problem here", only to find that the signpost to which he was referring (Lullington) was missing. "It was there a few days ago," he said.

I look forward to your comments.

Yours faithfully

Mike Carden
Founder Member, SPOGLITEC

I'm pleased to say that I even received a reply, which, whilst pointing out the difficulty of coping with a declining budget, also mentioned that High Ham was well worth seeing twice.

When I did finally find my way past High Ham and Henley, the road did become flat and straight – for the most part – with the road often raised above water-filled ditches on either side. The Somerset Levels are old peat marsh, where the rivers met the sea and constantly flooded back up the valleys. When they were drained to create farmland such as the King's Sedge Field, what was left was flat, except for the ridges separating the valleys. Those ridges were not high, but, well, I was starting to flake and the number of tissues I was getting through was increasing.

I had wasted a lot of time around High Ham, and was getting hungry again. I needed a refuelling stop, a couple of muesli bars perhaps. The sign for the Sweet Track and a nature reserve came at the right moment. I pulled in and re-fuelled, then scooted Scott around some little tracks to a notice board showing where the Sweet Track had been found.

In 1970 a peat-cutter by the name of Ray Sweet came across planks buried underground. Investigation showed that this was a walkway of oak, built to join the small islands nestling in the Somerset marshes before they were drained. Extraordinarily, the tree rings in the oak have been exactly matched to the year 3807BC. So 5,813 years ago, give or take a few months, a man had stood on the exact spot as me, contemplating where he and his mates were going to lay their walkway.

I like to feel connections like that. In one way it seems an eternity, almost impossible to comprehend. And yet that eternity might only equate to 290 generations. In terms of evolution, 290 generations is nothing. These were people like you and me. Though maybe handier with a flint axe.

High above, a buzzard was gliding.

I have had a thing about birds of prey since Claire and I lived in Birmingham. We were in our mid-twenties and staying for a while with Claire's mother. We were there in the run-up to Christmas and were invited round to a neighbour's house for a Christmas drink.

Now, I need you to imagine the scene. Joyce was thin, with permed, grey hair, and she welcomed us in from her seat at the Hammond organ, where she was playing with great gusto a selection of classics of the time – The Birdie Song, Ooh La Paloma Blanca and so on. The lounge-dining room was crowded with her friends, like her in middle to older stages of life, standing around drinking Brew XI or Babycham. On every surface and wall were mementos of holidays in Torremelinos and Fuengerola – castanets, flamenco dancers, brightly coloured fans.

Claire and I made our way through the throng to the dining room area and helped ourselves to drinks, where Joyce's husband Stan was standing talking to a lady sitting on a small settee. He was red-faced from plenty of Brew XI, his accent broad brummie. He said hello, raising his voice over the top of the singing around the Hammond organ.

Oh this year we're off to sunny Spain

"D'you wanna see me kistrel?"

Y viva espana

His kestrel? Who has a kestrel in deepest, darkest Birmingham?

We're taking the costa brava plane

"Yes. Please."

Y viva espana

He disappeared into the kitchen, and the lady on the settee exchanged blank looks with us.

If you'd like to chat a matador
In some cool cabana

When he came back, he had on his gloved hand the most

beautiful kestrel, eyes bright, feathers glossy, tallons sharp. He was talking to the bird, calming it amongst the noise.

And meet senoritas by the score

"This is Shoine."

Espana por favor

"Shane? Like in the cowboy film?"

OH this year we're off to sunny Spain

"Yes. Shoine."

Y viva espana

I became aware of a low moaning from the lady on the settee, and that she was holding up her arms to fend off the bird.

We're taking the costa brava plane

Stan leaned the kestrel closer to her. "D'you wanna tooch him?"

The lady threw herself face down on the settee with a long wail.

Y viva espana

Stan had obviously never come across anyone with a bird phobia.

If you'd like to chat a matador

He looked at us, bewildered.

In some cool cabana

The wail from the settee - *And meet senoritas by the score* - became teeth-jarringly high-pitched just as the singing reached its crescendo.

ESPANA POR FAVOR!

The singing stopped and the only sound was that long, piercing wail from the couch. I looked up and every single face around the organ was turned towards us.

From behind me a Brummie voice carried across the room. "D'you wanna see me boozard?"

Back in the present, I pedalled on, and a short way up the road, came to the Peat Moors Visitor Centre, which had been one of my targets when I started planning my route. I knew there was a reconstructed Iron Age village. What I also found was a reconstructed Iron Age garden centre with a reconstructed Iron Age café. Very advanced these Iron Age people. Anyway, I decided I needed some more refuelling.

I chained Scott to a post. "Stay, Scott, stay."

Watching me from the café were two cyclists, a man and a woman wearing almost-matching lycra bike shirts in blue and yellow with an array of adverts. Proper cyclists.

"Going far?" the man asked. He was older than me, maybe just retired.

I plonked my cup of tea on their table and joined them. "Well, today I started at Sherborne, and I'm going via Glastonbury to Street."

"So where are you ending up eventually?"

"Berwick-upon-Tweed."

"That's a good ride. What are you doing per day? 70? 80 miles?"

"Erm, no. About 40 actually. But I'm stopping off a lot."

The man was silent a while, and it was his wife who said, "That's a good idea."

"Where have you come from?" I asked.

"Weston," man-cyclist said. "It's just a little run out. About 40 miles."

"Oh."

"We're on a tandem."

A tandem, I had been told, was harder work than riding your own bike. It seemed these were fit people, and indeed they were. It turned out that they were retired, and spent a good part of each winter cycling in Spain.

"It's great country for cycling," man-cyclist said. "Long straight roads, and the car drivers treat you as proper road-users. Much better than here. The only thing you have to watch is when one of the Race Teams of cyclists overtake you. They train out there for the Tour de France and so on. You don't hear them coming and suddenly it's 'whoosh-

whoosh-whoosh' as they go past you. Mind you, we get some good speeds out there. Over 50 miles an hour once."

50? I only go above 30 when I'm cycling downhill with the wind behind me, and it feels incredibly fast. Wind in the hair and eyes, too noisy to hear, goose-pimples on the arms and legs. I couldn't conceive of 50 miles an hour on my bike.

At the Peat Moors Visitor Centre, Lorraine was on duty. She was wonderfully enthusiastic, and I guess that's what got her the job. She had started as a volunteer and now works there.

The compound had information boards relating the incredibly hard life of the peat-cutters and a reconstruction of the Sweet Track – cut branches buried in the ground in an X shape to carry oak planks.

I wandered across to the three large round huts, their thatched roofs reaching down low towards the ground. Lorraine was tending a fire on a stone hearth inside one of the huts.

"The smoke finds its way out through the thatch eventually," she said.

Today, though, the smoke was swirling around the dark hut, and we stood in the doorway to get air while she told me about the Trust which runs the centre.

"We get lots of school groups in," she said. "We show them how to make the wattle-and-daub walls." She pointed to a mud patch. "Bit messy sometimes, but good fun."

Now that sounded like a good school history trip: digging in a clay pit then smearing it on walls (and almost certainly each other).

The huts were based on archaeological evidence from digs on the peat moors. Iron age, so pre-Roman, but also very similar to what the people reverted to when the Roman Empire collapsed. I wonder how long the memory lasted of under-floor heating, of piped water, and of high-columned stone buildings?

I cycled on towards Glastonbury and soon had a hill with a tower on it as my target. Glastonbury Tor. In the sunshine.

The town of Glastonbury was busy. A nice atmosphere, and I left Scott chained to a lamppost while I had a look around. It was a little hard to comprehend the mixture of 'new age' and 'old age': ringleted hippies carried babies, and grey-haired ladies carried shopping; a shop called 'Hemp of Avalon' stood cheek-by-jowl with 'The George and Pilgrim' pub; and around the corner from the ruins of what had been the second largest monastery in England are shops called 'Birth of Venus' and 'Earth Goddess'.

Several shops also had maps showing the ley lines which apparently link ancient lines of power in the earth, and many of them emanate from Glastonbury. A map costs just £3.99. Better value than an Ordnance Survey map, I would say.

I was torn though. Another map showed how the area around Glastonbury mirrors the signs of the zodiac in the sky. I seemed to have cycled through Gemini and Leo, and was standing in Aquarius. It was obviously too hard a choice to make, so I went and sat in the sun.

Glastonbury is known for its 'alternative' culture and for its Festival (though that isn't in the town itself at all), but for a thousand years it was one of the most important centres of Christianity in England. The first documentary evidence is for a church in 601AD. Through the next few hundred years gifts from pilgrims and the nobility made the monastery grow and prosper.

The pilgrims came to Glastonbury because of the legends attached to the site. The oldest of the legends concerns Joseph of Arimethea, a disciple of Jesus, or possibly his uncle. He apparently came to this small hamlet surrounded by salt marshes, bringing with him either the Holy Grail or two vials of Jesus's blood – depending on which version of the legend we run with. Later versions also include Joseph's staff taking root in the soil and growing. Puritans would later cut down the original tree, but the thorn tree behind the abbey ruins is said to be a descendant of that very staff.

The legend grew – even after the monastery was no more – and a new version added that Joseph had brought a young Jesus here. And it is this legend that was used by William Blake, and which is still sung with fervour by the unlikely pairing of football fans and the Women's Institute:

And did those feet in ancient time
Walk upon England's mountains green?
And was the Holy Lamb of God
On England's pleasant pastures seen?

Then the bit we can't remember
And then, altogether now:

*Till we have **built Jerooosalem***
In England's green and pleasant land.

I hummed it. Quietly.

There's another legend intimately bound up with Glastonbury. King Arthur. There have been so many versions of the Arthurian legends, placing him all across the country. One substantial thread named Glastonbury as the famed Isle of Avalon. And it must be true – the sign on the main road into Glastonbury calls the town 'the ancient Avalon'.

In the 12th century the abbey church was burned to the ground, and the monks used the opportunity to follow up a story that had been passed to them that King Arthur and Guinevere were buried in the grounds.

The monks dug down, and – miraculously – found a grave stone with these words: HIC IACET SEPULTUS INCLITUS REX ARTURIUS IN INSULA AVALONIA. Or: Here lies buried the renowned King Arthur in the Isle of Avalon.

Two sets of bones were found below – a tall man killed by a blow to the head, and a shorter body with the remains of long blond hair.

It does sound as though Glastonbury Abbey had employed its own advertising team.

With these powerful legends, pilgrims and their gifts poured in. Glastonbury vied with Westminster Abbey in terms of wealth, and that wealth was used to build a truly vast abbey church – 550 foot or 167m long. It also housed a library of irreplaceable documents – royal and religious charters through centuries. And it all came to nothing.

Glastonbury Abbey was one of many monasteries and nunneries across England, and by the 16th century the abbeys owned a very large amount of property. So wealthy did the monasteries become, that when there was a King of England bold enough, avaricious enough, and bad enough, the monasteries stood no chance.

If it had not been Henry VIII, another bold, avaricious, bad King would no doubt have come along, but it is Henry we can blame.

The dissolution of Glastonbury's monastery was not so different from many others across England. It was bloody, brutal and destructive.

Abbot Whiting of Glastonbury was eighty years old when Henry's men came to arrest him for high treason and carry him off to the Tower of London. He was, according to those arresting him, "a very weak man and sickly".

The 47 monks were thrown out of their lodgings to make their own way in the world. That left the abbey open to official looting. "We have found," Henry's men wrote, "a fair chalice of gold, and divers other parcels of plate."

At his trial in Wells, the abbot would not admit to treason, but there was to be no mercy. The old man was dragged through the streets, beheaded, and his head was displayed on the gate of the abbey. His body was then cut into quarters and each part was sent to a separate part of Somerset.

The library's precious, irreplaceable, historical documents were scattered and largely destroyed. The lead was removed from the roof and sold, while the walls were used as a quarry.

What did I call Henry? Bold, avaricious, and bad. I'm probably being too kind to him.

I turned my attention to the tower on the hill. Though it must be said that I was not feeling too well by now. I was getting through an awful lot of tissues as my runny nose clicked into a higher gear.

Scott and I followed signs to the tor and we instead found ourselves in a housing estate half-way up the side of a hill.

I blamed Scott.

Back down at the entrance to the housing estate, we came across a very obvious footpath with a sign for the tor, which, as I pointed out, any self-respecting mountain bike should have seen.

A stile and footpath led steeply up through a field. Of the tor itself, there was no sign.

"You're not going to make it up there," I said.

"I'll wait."

I chained him to a rusty gate that had not been opened in many a year, and realised that the house by the gate had a row of Tibetan prayer wheels along its wall. I turned them and they made a gentle sound which seemed to fit somehow with the religious mix that is now Glastonbury.

With the sun on my back, I made my way up, and a glimpse through the hedge showed me the tor discouragingly far off. Behind me, the town sat in a haze, and the Somerset Levels merged into the distance. Finally the view opened up in front of me across a field of white and yellow flowers to the tower on the hill. It was, well, enchanting. And I was shattered. I never did make it to the top. I took a photograph and went back down to Scott.

"That was quick," he said.

The road to Street turned out to be flat, with much of it on a cycle lane. Unfortunately, the road from the town up to the Youth Hostel was steep and long, and I got to thinking about chafing.

I had had a conversation with Steve along the lines of -

Steve: "Do you have Vaseline?"

Me: "Vaseline?"

Steve: "For the chafing. You know - saddle, tops of legs, sore. All that." And he had gestured towards where a person might develop soreness when on a saddle for a long time.

Me: "Oh. I'll be fine."

As I cycled up that long hill, it occurred to me that I was cycling with my knees turned outwards so as to prevent further chafing of the now rather raw region gestured to by my brother, and that really I should have brought some Vaseline. But I did, though, have something else. Something passed to me by Claire as I was setting out, in case my lips should get too dry.

I dug into a pannier. I had with me a small pot of '**Mediterranean Olive, Sage and Almond WONDER-BALM** with skin-nourishing ORGANIC olive oil, fragrant sage oil and ORGANIC sweet almond oil'. Fabulous.

I was destined from now, I realised, to start each day's ride with my crotch nourished, fragranced and sweetened with Olive, Sage and Almond WONDERBALM, and the world should surely be grateful for that.

Street was a company town, full of Clarks Shoes factories in the days when England was the factory for the world. Today those factories are closed, and part of the land is now the hugely popular Clarks Factory Outlet. The youth hostel was originally built by Clarks as a recuperation home for its staff, and they built it away from the smoke, on the top of a hill. Curse them.

The YHA man was very welcoming and the hostel had a nice feel to it. It was a traditional hostel – solid wood doors, OS maps on the walls and no television. Incongruously, it also had a brand new computerised booking system, and my host could see from the coloured blocks on his screen that I was one of just four staying on this Monday pre-summer-holiday night.

"I might as well give you a dormitory to yourself," he said.

I sniffed. "Yes, Good idea."

Scott and I made our way round to the bike shed, where it seemed he had company.

"No parties," I said.

Upstairs in my very own dormitory I chose a bottom bunk and wrestled the strange elongated sheet-sleeping-bag into place. I'm not sure why the YHA still favours these. They are double the length of a bed, so the idea is that they fold at the bottom of the bunk, with one half underneath you, and one half over you, covered by the duvet. They are not quite wide enough to tuck in properly on either side, which is all very well if you don't wriggle about in your sleep, but not ideal if you do. I would suggest to the YHA that in a time of computerised booking services, maybe the sheet sleeping bag has had its day.

Somehow my panniers exploded all over the floor and neighbouring bunks as I searched for a towel and non-cycling clothes. It was when I found my non-cycling trousers that I felt in the pocket a small square-ish item. I knew straightaway what it was, and I thought of the scene at Sherborne all those miles ago when I was searching hopelessly for my bike computer. I sat down fairly heavily on the bed, and squashed the sandwiches left over from lunch time.

YHA Hostels sell basic provisions for those with squashed sandwiches. Well, usually they do.

I parked myself at a table in the dining room to read a book and to eat squashed sandwiches.

I was found there by the three other people staying – all men of a certain age on long-distance bike rides. There was something interesting about that, although slightly alarming.

We talked about our routes. One was cycling from Land's End to Bath. The other two from Dorset to Lancashire. Why were there four middle-aged men here pedalling for hundreds of miles across England? Were we all cycling in search of the Meaning of Life? Or at least the Meaning of Mid-Life? I didn't say "Mid-Life Crisis" out loud of course. That wouldn't have been very English.

Besides, I had something almost as frightening to worry about. The very real possibility that I was in the early stages of, whisper it quietly, Man-Flu.

Captain's log: Day Two
The day's distance: approximately 45 miles / 72Km
The journey so far: 94.89 miles / 151.82Km
Average speed: no idea
Maximum speed: no idea
Nose: running

Day Three

Target: 36 miles from Street to Bradford on Avon, via Wells and Farleigh Castle

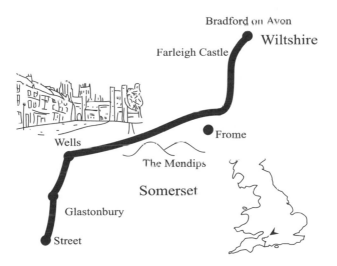

I didn't sleep well. I coughed and spluttered and fought with my sheet-sleeping-bag. I was very grateful not to be sharing a dormitory with the other epic cyclists. Not as glad as they were though.

With a long ride downhill and then a flat cycle back to Glastonbury I felt better. Tissues were strategically placed. The day was dry and there were glimpses of sunshine. I would make it to Bradford on Avon and some home-cooking from my parents. I would be fine.

The road through Glastonbury to Wells was straightforward according to the map. So I only got a little lost.

And once out of Glastonbury on the right road, an NCN cycle route appeared, heading my way, off on to an absolutely straight and flat route across the Levels. I overtook a jogger, probably the first 'Glastonbury-alternative-lifestyle-jogger' I had seen, with his blond dreadlocks bouncing along. When I stopped for a drink, he ran past me.

"Hi," I said.

He ignored me. Maybe I wasn't alternative enough.

I came to a fork where the NCN route went right and my map suggested left. Here is the problem with the NCN signing. Mostly, the signs simply have a number, and don't say where they are leading to. If you don't have the correct NCN map for that route, you don't know if – for example – the sign will take you on a delightful back route into Wells, or lead you in the opposite direction.

My Zen route-finding suggested that I go left and not follow the NCN route. I ended up on the dual carriage-way.

When I did manage to find my way into Wells itself, I loved it. A long street of shops led into a market place busy with shoppers, tourists and the odd film crew.

"What are you filming?" I asked a young lady with a clipboard and a serious expression.

She didn't make eye contact. "A comedy."

"For the TV?"

"No. Feature film."

"Ooh. Do you want an extra on a bike?" I gestured at Scott. He gestured at me.

"No," she said.

The conversation, it seemed, was at an end. Their loss, I think you will agree.*

What I really liked about the market place was the outside of the shops and banks. The council must have stipulated that businesses must not rip out the frontages and replace them with awful modern monstrosities. So the town still had character. Huge character. One of the big banks still had its original bow windows. In which case, perhaps they might care to reinstate some frontages in other towns they have mangled? Dispense with the plastic? Please.

I bought brunch from a baker's, and, at the far end of the market place, found the arch leading through into the cathedral precinct. The cathedral was something I had been looking forward to, particularly the view of the front. A bench was free so I brunched and took it all in.

The front of the church is astonishing, 150 feet wide and 100 feet high, with about 300 carved biblical figures. Many of these figures are over human height. In their natural mellow-gold stone, they are beautiful. As they were 800 years ago

*I later discovered they had been filming 'Hot Fuzz'.

they would have been astonishing, because a visitor then would not have seen the mellow-gold stone. Each figure would have been painted – bright blues, rich purples and deep greens, with edging and crowns in gold leaf, all set against a dark red for each stone niche.

I remember going to the cinema to see Star Wars, and the wonder of that opening shot – the space craft coming in over the heads of the audience, and just going on and on. I had never seen anything like that before. How much more wonder would come over a 13th century peasant on a trip into market when he saw Wells Cathedral for the first time – the saints and kings in 150 foot-wide Cinemascope. It's hard to take in the utter astonishment that he or she must have felt.

Then maybe the peasant would go inside, just as I did, and the wonder would go on. Wells Cathedral is gob-smackingly beautiful. Great pillars rise up on either side taking the eyes upwards where the ribs of the pillars splay out across the roof. I dropped my eyes and found them resting on an enormous curvy "scissor-arch" that crosses from one side to the other. It surely cannot be original. It's too modern, too sensuous for those days. And indeed it was not built in the 13th century like the rest of the cathedral. No, it was built in the 15th century when some of the pillars started sinking. It worked. The cathedral is still standing. Still beautiful. They knew how to build in those days.

It has always amazed me that the masons, architects, planners and first builders of the great cathedrals of the middle ages must have known that they would never live to see their work finished. How many people these days will work like that, accepting that they will only see part-built walls, scaffolding, plain unpainted stone? Not the glorious building that would amaze the locals of the following generation.

I was not alone in the cathedral of course. There were the usual parties of school-children and the tourists who had paid £5 a head to go in. I realised that they were beginning to congregate in one place, looking up. High on a wall, knights on horse-back looked ready for a tournament. A bell rang and the tournament started, the knights jousting as they had every fifteen minutes for centuries, this being the third oldest clock in Europe. On the hour, I gathered, one of the figures kicks the bell. Well, so would I after all that time.

Outside the cathedral I followed signs for the Vicars Close, and another arch led me into a street of low houses with high chimneys. Inside one of the houses, a violin played a gentle melody. The street would have been lovely if it were not bin-day. All along the road, black bin bags ruined the symmetry.

I could have stayed much longer in Wells, but it was time to go. I bought what would be Lunch 2 at the same bakers, Mentho-Lyptus and tissues in the chemists, and set off to conquer the Mendip Hills. I say 'set off' but of course there was the familiar cycle around the town vainly looking for a signpost before centrifugal force finally threw me out on what I hoped was the right route.

The Mendips were shockingly high. Perhaps my cold didn't help, but the hill seemed huge, and each time I reached the top and stopped (to admire the view), another top appeared. The view, though, was a good one – all the way back to Glastonbury Tor poking up from the flat Levels. It seemed a good idea to stop several times to admire the view.

Once at the top of the Mendips the land was quite different. There were missing signposts again, and a missing turn-off, but I followed a straight road which rolled up and down along the ridge, before it finally dropped into Mells.

A stone shelter next to a duck-pond and a village shop seemed ideal for Lunch 2, and I watched the comings and goings of the little community before having a stroll around. A map of the village gave a brief history. Mells had been a wool-town, like so many here, and had belonged to Glastonbury Abbey.

In the churchyard is the grave of a former inhabitant,

Little Jack Horner, no longer in his corner, eating his pudding and pie. Local legend, disputed by Jack's descendents, is that the original Jack Horner was the last steward of Glastonbury Abbey, and that he was sent to Henry VIII to offer him the deeds to ten manors as a peace offering. The deeds were hidden inside a pie in case of highwaymen, until Jack put in his thumb and pulled out 'the plumb' for himself - Mells Manor.

More missed turns (aarrghh!) and I found my way past the village of Rode. There used to be Bird Gardens at Rode, and I can vividly remember the day as a child that I learned not to put a finger up to a parrot cage. The parrot grabbed and held on, while my parents and friends flocked around. I don't like parrots. Well, not close up.

On the steep hill up from Tellisford, a man was leaning on his bike.

"Hallo," I said.

He flinched, not having heard me toiling up the hill to pass him. "Oi norrrmally push up the wassnames," he said, his accent telling me I was back in Wiltshire, where I grew up.

"I don't blame you."

The country had changed again, with the hedgerows hugging the edges of the roads. There were more trees here – ash, oak, chestnut and more. I could remember the year that Dutch Elm Disease took out all the elms, and dead trees stood in rows alongside fields. Now they are long gone, but this part of Wiltshire always seems full of woods, and I like that.

It was mid-afternoon now, and quite hot, when Farleigh Hungerford Castle appeared.

"Ice cream, Scott?"

"Oh yes, very comical."

There is not a great deal left of Sir Thomas Hungerford's 14th century castle now. Most of its walls are beaten down, its towers crumbling, and I was ready to be disappointed when signs led me into the chapel. Here, though, high up on the walls are medieval paintings of George and the Dragon. The chapel had once been the village's church, but Sir Thomas's son had extended the walls of the castle to include the church. The church became the castle's chapel, with family tombs in a side-chapel, coats of arms on the walls, and St George doing his mythical stuff with the dragon.

It seems the Hungerford family were not necessarily the ideal family men either. The Ladies Tower was evidently used to incarcerate the wife of one of the lords of the manor, and she was only kept alive by locals climbing ladders to the window and pushing food through.

Food. Yes. Time to go on to Bradford on Avon.

The clouds gathered as I left the castle and negotiated the hills leading into Wiltshire. Two counties down. Ten to go. Tomorrow would be Avebury, Devizes and Cricklade. Deepest Wiltshire, then on to Gloucestershire, if I made it that far. There were long days to come – 51 miles tomorrow if I had my distances right. So maybe nearer 60 if previous experience was anything to go by. Also, I didn't like the look of the blackening sky.

The rain started just before I arrived in Bradford.

We'd moved to Bradford on Avon in 1969 from Saltash in Cornwall, when I was ten years old. My mother took me in to my new school. I distinctly remember my nervousness and Mrs Coleman looking me in the eyes and saying, "Hello Michael." I said, "I've got my pencil case," and Mrs Coleman smiled as if that was all that mattered.

Bradford on Avon was very different to Saltash for me. My dad had been at Devonport Dockyard for the regulation Ministry of Defence three years, when they told him that he would be moving to Bath. Saltash was a good place to live for my three older brothers. They could go climbing and canoeing, play tennis or football. But I was lonely there, living a couple of miles from my school and friends.

Bradford instantly felt like home. We lived a few hundred yards from the school. There were children all around, and there was a playing field up the road. It was ten-year-old heaven.

To an extent, Bradford still feels like home, even though I have not lived there for many years. It has lost something and gained something in the intervening time. With the closure of the Avon Rubber Company in town, it has lost some of its realness, but it has gained, somehow, beauty. I would, I thought, struggle to find a town more beautiful than Bradford on Avon during my ride north.

The old sign at the entrance to the town says:

BRADFORD ON AVON
SAXON CHURCH
CHAPEL ON THE BRIDGE
TITHE BARN
ST MARY'S, TORY

Next to it is a newer sign that says:

HUMPS

This five-strong list of Bradford's highlights hardly does justice to a town which nestles into the hillside. Arrayed across the slope above the river are weavers' cottages, Georgian mansions, churches and a round house, all in magnificent, golden Bath-stone.

I cycled past the pub from where the motor bike gang had chased us as fifteen-year-old lads, when we'd tried to buy our halves of lager-and-lime. We'd finally lost them amongst the alleyways and steps on the far side of the river, their motorbikes failing to follow where our scooters, bikes and legs had led.

On past the sign for the huge medieval tithe barn, which was then used to store high-sided farm wagons, perfect for canoodling teenagers to get out of the rain.

I'll call her Mary. That's not her real name, of course, but I feel the need to protect the identity of the innocent, or in this case the guilty. I had asked Mary to walk down with me to the school disco. She had said she would meet me there, but arrived on the arm of another boy. I feel no animosity of course, not thirty years later. I have, as I am sure you can tell, virtually forgotten the humiliation of a fourteen-year-old lad dumped by his girlfriend in full view of every other child in the school. Virtually, anyway.

And past the road where the grammar school had stood. 'Fitzmaurice' it had been named, after its founder, with the four houses named for other worthies. There was the manly-sounding 'Blake' which won everything, and the slightly less manly-sounding 'Pinkney' that was my house, and that didn't win anything.

"Pinkney?" Scott said.

"Yes, I know. They've a lot to answer for."

Past the pretty alms houses and the stately golden Westbury House with its Georgian windows. Over the medieval bridge with its 'chapel' that was really a lock-up for medieval drunks. I'm sure there are still some medieval drunks in most towns.

Past the empty shell of the Avon Rubber Company factory, still waiting for its renovation and Luxury Apartments with River View.

Past The Shambles, and up into Bradford's hills.

My legs and nose were fighting back now. This was too much, especially in the growing rain. Slowly up Silver Street. Even more slowly up Frying Pan Hill.

"Frying Pan?"

"Yes, Scott. Frying Pan."

"No."

"Yes."

Left up New Road, right, past my old junior school, and finally I was there at my parents' house, where I had grown up. Shattered. Absolutely shattered. This was not Man-Flu, I said to myself. It couldn't be. No, all I needed was a really good cup of tea.

Captain's log: Day Three
The day's distance: 40.96 miles / 65.54Km
The journey so far: 135.85 miles / 217.36Km
Average speed: 11.6mph / 18 56Kmph
Maximum speed: 33.5mph / 53.6Kmph

"Hello, Dad. Hello, Mum."
"Hello, Michael," Mum said. "Cup of tea?"

Day Four

**Target: 51 miles from Bradford on Avon to Cricklade,
via Devizes and Avebury**

Bradford on Avon

51 miles. That was the target anyway.

I woke full of cold at 5.50am. No, I'm wrong. It was not a cold. This was proper Man-Flu. Women always seem to snigger at men with Man-Flu, while they soldier on through colds, flu, pneumonia, scurvy, plague and so on. I intend to write a scientific paper proving that Man-Flu must be treated by full bed-rest with the television remote control in reach.

The weather forecast had been for heavy rain to arrive mid-morning, and I had intended to get up early so as to get plenty of miles covered before the deluge. But this, as I say, was proper Man-Flu. I blew my nose hugely several times, shaking the house slightly, sucked two Mentho-Lyptus, and put my head back on the pillow. When I next opened my eyes, it was 9.30, and I felt rotten.

Ironically, the weather was not too bad to start with. If I had been well enough, and had got up at 5.50, I could have done an awful lot of the mileage in reasonable weather. I had been going to cycle the Kennet and Avon Canal towpath to Devizes in time for brunch, then take to the hills to get to the dramatic Avebury stone circle, and on to finish at Cricklade north of Swindon. A long day, but possible, and I really wanted to go to Avebury.

I had been there any number of times when I was young, but none since I had heard an interview on the television with a large man, full-bearded and wearing a long, grey-white, cloaky thing.

"I am the Druid Keeper of the Stones," he had told the interviewer. "My name is Terry."

Fabulous. You couldn't make it up. The Druid Keeper of the Stones is not Llewellyn, or Diarmaid, or Cadwaladr, or some other Druidic-sounding name, but Terry.

Terry is a figure of some controversy, though it must be said that the controversy comes from different sides.

I did a search on the internet on *Terry Druid Avebury* and

came up with a vibrant discussion on the merits and de-merits of Terry having been given the key to the gate at Silbury Hill (a few miles from Avebury) by English Heritage and allowed to climb to conduct his ceremonies. Most of the discussion was critical, but from a variety of viewpoints. Damaging the hill. Causing cars to swerve. Giving Pagans a bad name. Encouraging crop-circle spotters to climb the hill. Giving Pagans a good name. That sort of thing.

I think he's great. Someone in that fine tradition of mild British eccentricity. Terry, if you're out there, all the best, mate. I had hoped to bump in to you while you were Keeping the Stones, but it was not to be. Another time.

Instead, we went to the supermarket, and I bought two boxes of tissues and two packets of Mentho-Lyptus – the EXTRA-STRONG variety.

I called at the station and found I could get to Cheltenham by train the following day, half way through Day Five's route. That would have to do. I'd be better by then. Please.

Back at my parents' house, I set to thinking about Bradford on Avon. In most towns, you can say to yourself, hm, Georgian, or Tudor, or Victorian, or even the dreaded 1960s. Bradford on Avon, though, has a whole range of buildings reflecting most of the different ages of English history, though the earliest are hidden.

Bradford is built either side of a river – the 'broad ford' of the town's name – and runs up the side of the hill on one side, spilling over the top. On the top was an Iron Age hill-fort, and after that had been abandoned, there was a Roman villa. Recent excavations have uncovered mosaic floors. These have been covered over after each dig, since the remains are under the school playing fields. It wouldn't do for the Romans to interfere with football matches.

Then we come to the buildings that you can still see. First there is the Saxon church, used as a private house until a vicar in the 19th century realised what he was looking at. Today it's a high-roomed, stone building. Dark and atmospheric.

There were probably two Saxon churches, with the other being replaced by Holy Trinity church in Norman times, and added to with passing generations. Jump on to the 14th century and there is the stone tithe-barn, built to take in the tithe (or 10% of produce) to be paid to the owners of the town – the nunnery at Shaftesbury. The tithe-barn is truly enormous, heavy stone walls supporting a vast structure of wooden beams and stone roof slates. There are two great double doors on each side, wide enough for wagons to have brought in grain or wool for storage.

Bradford became rich on the proceeds of wool, and the town still has the cottages of weavers and the mansions of the wool merchants. When the industrial revolution came, Bradford had riots as workers lost their skilled jobs to machines in the 'manufactories' – the mill buildings which are also still here. Wool had its day though, and the mill buildings were converted to the rubber industry in the 19th century and to apartments in the 20th century.

The latest industry to take over the town is tourism – visitors come to see all these sublime buildings huddling together, in mellow golden stone.

You could, I thought, write the history of England by writing the history of Bradford on Avon. I wasn't quite up to that. Not with Man-Flu.

Captain's log: Day Four
The day's distance: 0 miles / 0Km
The journey so far: still 139.85 miles / 223.76Km
Average speed: 0 mph / 0 Kmph
Maximum speed: 0 mph / 0 Kmph
Me: holding up heroically under truly rampant Man-Flu

Day Five

Target: 25 miles from Cheltenham to the Malvern Hills, via Deerhurst

Ledbury

The Malvern Hills

Deerhurst

Gloucestershire

Cheltenham

Rampant Man-Flu does not disappear overnight, but we men are of course well-known as a resilient lot. Besides, the sun was flitting out from behind clouds from time to time and, truthfully, it felt right to be on the move again.

I oiled the bike-chain.

"About time."

"Alright."

Apart from the gears sticking, Scott had behaved himself.

"Every day please."

"If I must."

"I don't ask for much."

"Wouldn't be much point if you did."

I said goodbye to my mum and dad, the last family I would see until Northumberland, when Claire would bring 14-year-old Richard across to join me for the last few days. Northumberland seemed a long way off.

I cycled down to Bradford on Avon's station, stocking up on cold relief, more tissues and more EXTRA-STRONGs on the way. A train to Bristol and another to Cheltenham, and I was nearly back on the route. A day and a half, and Terry, missed.

I had a strangely familiar feeling as I sat on the bike outside Cheltenham station. That 'lost' sort of feeling.

Why do people turn signs round? What pleasure do they get? Anyway, several sets of directions later, and I was on a minor road going north past Staverton. It was flat, which was good. It was not raining, which was also good. And beyond Boddington someone had planted hundreds of trees parallel with the road, mostly horse chestnuts. There were cream and pink blossoms from the trees, set against the green of meadows or the bright yellow of rape fields. It was a picture.

There was no sign for the left turn I was looking for, and I flew past, but I wouldn't blame Gloucestershire County Council too much. The road didn't really lead to anywhere other than the A38. Beyond that however, there were signs for Deerhurst. The tiny hamlet is at the end of two lanes which lead nowhere else. It is a backwater. Quite literally a backwater, in fact, because the Severn runs just behind the village and there are flood gates to prevent a deluge.

Deerhurst has not always been such a haven of peace and quiet. There are two Anglo-Saxon churches here and there was a Treaty of Deerhurst, again in Saxon times. The treaty was between the marvellously named King Edmund Ironside and the Danish King Cnut, the leader of an invading Viking army. But in the same year – 1016 – Edmund died, and Cnut became King of England as well as Denmark. We tend to remember him as King Canute, and we remember him as the King who could not hold back the tide, rather than the leader of a successful Viking invasion of England.

I left Scott at the gate to the parish church, prettily placed in its churchyard with a tudor house off to one side. In the church, a lady was setting flowers for her god-daughter's wedding.

The church is what is left of an Anglo-Saxon monastery, with some stonework from 700AD. Very early as stone churches go. Before that date, most churches would have been wooden.

The church itself is tall, as the Saxons liked them, two stories high. It would have been narrow, but in medieval times side aisles were added to give more space and light. You can still imagine how the original church must have been though – a rectangular box of a building with small triangular-topped windows high up in the walls.

The walls today are a mix of white-wash and stone. Any original decoration, such as the curly stone carvings on the font and the almost boggle-eyed angel outside, don't feel 'English' somehow. But there is a reason for that. When the Normans came, almost all the Anglo-Saxon churches were destroyed and replaced by 'modern' buildings using architectural ideas and designs from France – the cathedrals, abbeys and parish churches that we think of as quintessentially 'English' today. Where there is a remaining pre-Norman church, such as Deerhurst – for all that it is small and obscure – it is a treasure.

After Cnut's death, the throne of England reverted to English hands, and it was the reign of Edward the Confessor that was referred to in the carved stone found 900 years later in Deerhurst: 'Earl Odda ordered this royal hall to be built in the fourteenth year of Edward, King of the English', ie 1056, ten years before English history would change forever.

Odda also built a chapel, a building that was used as a farm outbuilding until the 19th century, until the local vicar recognised it. The story is so similar to the story of Bradford on Avon's Saxon Church, that you wonder if there are more out there unrecognised.

Odda's Chapel is owned by English Heritage. I walked around to it, and found a stone building snuggling up to a black-and-white timber house. The inside of the chapel was quite bare though, and I walked back up to the parish church to have lunch on the bench outside.

As I ate, the rain came on again, so I moved Scott under a tree, and went back inside for a second look.

"You're working hard," I said to the lady cutting flowers and branches.

"I'll have help tomorrow. The main flowers will come then. Today is mostly the branches."

"Branches?"

"Yes, the colour scheme of the wedding is brown, lightened with cream and orange. We've been gathering things through the winter."

"It'll look beautiful," I said. And it would. The church would come to life with a wedding, and flowers, and people.

"Thank you," she said.

The rain eased, and I went back out to Scott. I wheeled him back to the lane, where a postman was delivering. He looked at my panniers and said, "I don't envy you the hill."

"Hill?" I said.

"Hill?" Scott said – though more quietly than I did.

The postman laughed and drove off.

There was a hill, though not a massive one. We'd done much worse, and would do very, very much worse. You could tell this postman wasn't a cycling one.

A bridge took us over the River Severn and now we were in the land of proper black-and-white timber-framed buildings, suddenly quite different from the counties I had been through so far. The river felt like a border between the south-west and the midlands. We were getting north, Scott and me.

The first proper ups and downs came as I moved away from the valley of the Severn. In the distance I could see the Malvern Hills strung across the horizon, green and inviting. Somewhere in there was the hostel I was heading towards. This wasn't a YHA hostel. There wasn't one around here. No, this was a private one I had found on the internet.

I didn't know much about the hostel, but I knew it didn't do food, so when I passed a shop I bought myself a ready-meal and some fruit. The fruit looked more appetising than the ready-meal, but I would need something to eat later.

Warm sun alternated with heavy downpours accompanied by a cold wind as I made my way to the hostel. The Malverns were gradually getting bigger as I got closer. I was slowing down, tiring, and the sunny intervals had been reduced to sunny spells. A few miles short of the hostel, the sun vanished. The showers had finally amalgamated into a cold wet evening. I had my waterproof jacket on, but not my water-proof trousers or overshoes – I was saving these for really wet weather when the condensation inside would be preferable to the rain outside. But the short sharp showers had made my bottom half very wet.

At a homely-looking pub, I turned on to the road that would lead me up into the gap through the Malvern Hills where the hostel should lie, and the heavens opened. I pulled off the road to shelter under a hopelessly un-shelterable hedge, and watched as the wind whipped the branches around my head. The road ahead stretched upwards. Possibly a long upwards.

There were sheep ahead of me on the road – an A-road – and a farmer in a 4-wheel-drive shepherded them past me. I'd have liked a lift really, but that wasn't in the scheme of things. I sucked an EXTRA-STRONG, blew my nose and waited.

I gave up waiting for the rain to stop in the end and just waited for it to ease. When I gave up waiting for it to ease, I set off.

Thunder rolled down the hill towards me.

There are different techniques for hill-climbing on a bike. Some people rush at them whole-heartedly, legs pounding, heart pounding, until they either reach the top or suddenly have to stop before they expire. Others stand up on the pedals – push, push, push – eyes goggling, will-power taking them up. Another means is the 'slow and steady', inching up the hill, maybe zig-zagging across the road to cut down the steepness, getting there in the end.

My choice depends partly on whether I can see the top or not. If I can see the top, and think I can make it, I will go for it, head down, and hope for the best. The exception is if my knee is feeling wobbly, and I take it easy.

If I can't see the top, I'm definitely a 'slow and steady'. The top of this hill was a long way off, but in any case, I had no choice. My legs couldn't have pounded or pushed anywhere.

By the time I reached the hostel, I was dog-tired and very wet. I'd read Bill Bryson's 'Neither Here Nor There' recently, and one of the things that struck me was his arriving at an unknown town, and booking in to the most likely looking hotel. I particularly liked his phrase, 'It was expensive but spotless'. Not that all of them were that, of course. I think there was 'charming and reasonably priced', for example. But what I really wanted right now was 'expensive but spotless'.

As I ran the bike into a courtyard with a house on the left and sheds opposite, the rain stopped, a dog barked, and a lady appeared.

"Hello," she said. "Cup of tea?"

Oh yes, I thought. Oh yes, tea, food, shower, telly, warmth, anything.

She invited me into her kitchen, where tea from my host was followed by more tea from my host.

"Can I," I asked, "put my bike in one of the sheds?"

She looked at me, and I realised that the sheds were the hostel. This was not going to be 'expensive but spotless'. This was 'cheap and basic'. Very basic.

My host guided me to one of the sheds. It had white-washed breeze-block walls and a corrugated iron roof. There were two bunk-rooms. I chose one. Scott chose the other.

The bunks were squeezed in to low-ceilinged corners, and I laid out a sleeping bag the lady had brought in for me. Heat came from a tiny, noisy air-blower on the wall.

To get to the kitchen involved going out of one door into an open-air porch and into another door. OK when it wasn't raining hard.

Nobody else was staying in the hostel at all and I had my food alone in the kitchen. I heated up the ready-meal in a microwave. Cheesy, pasta-y thing. I burned it. It was horrid. Then I had a tomato cup-a-soup. So that was much better.

There was no telly, but a small radio tuned to talk-sport and the prospects for the England football team in the World Cup. I didn't bother trying to re-tune the radio – football talk is usually fine by me, and the alternatives weren't appetising. Radio 1 is a foreign language to me. Radio 2 in the evening seems to slide back through time to the 1950s. Radio 3 is a different foreign language. Radio 4 was likely to be The Archers and then something a little too worthy. And, judging by the reception, Radio 5 in the evenings is broadcast from the dark side of the moon. So I listened to the prattling as I ate.

Outside, the sun was trying to shine in a last evening's burst, and I phoned home sitting on a damp bench. The reception on my mobile was bad. Claire and I struggled to hear each other.

I had an early night. I'd looked at the map and tomorrow was going to have lots of contours. Tomorrow, I thought, I would be better and the sun would shine on me. I fell asleep listening to sheep through the walls warbling like the sound of an incoming message on my phone.

Captain's log: Day Five
The day's distance: 26.35 miles / 42.16 Km
The journey so far: 162.2 miles / 259.52 Km
Average speed: 10.3 mph / 16.48 Kmph
Maximum speed: 27.0 mph / 43.20 Kmph
Frame of mind: Just why was I here?

Day Six

Target: 35 miles from the Malvern Hills to Ludlow, via Ledbury, Bromyard and Tenbury

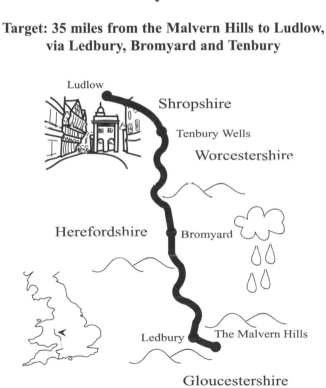

A friend once told me the story of his landlord and the landlord's architect.

The landlord had shown the architect a tiny cupboard and told him to design a shower-room and toilet to fit in it.

"Not possible," said the architect.

"If it's possible, I'll add 10% to your bill."

It had been possible, though very difficult to swing a cat in there.

This shower-room and toilet was smaller than that. Sitting on the loo, my knees were pressed firmly against the door and the sink was over my lap. I'm fairly sure that no architect had ever been near the place, but I would like to nominate it as the smallest bathroom in the world.

I hadn't slept brilliantly and, to be honest, I felt wrecked. Using the small, mottled mirror, I scraped stubble from my chin. I'd had a beard until a couple of years before, but gradually my brown hair had turned grey and my beard had developed whitey-grey patches amongst the brown. I'd finally decided that the 18-year-old beard had to go when one day I looked in the mirror and realised that I was now half-man, half-badger.

'Batman' works, I'd thought. 'Spiderman' works. But 'Badgerman'? I'd shaved my beard off before the rest of the family woke up.

As I'd cut and scraped, a long-hidden face had appeared. One that I recognised as my brother's, which was a little disconcerting.

When my three kids got up, one walked right past me and asked Claire when Uncle Andy had arrived. The second screamed and ran to fetch my third, who just stood there open-mouthed.

It hadn't been a good start to a new, beardless life.

The face in the mirror in the hostel in the Malvern Hills looked older than it should. There were wrinkles around the eyes, and the hair just shouldn't be grey. Dammit, my brain was not grey. Actually it probably was, but it still shouldn't be.

I added it to my Meaning of Mid-Life ponderings, rinsed my face and went to look at the sky in the gap between the bunkhouse and the kitchen. It was grey and windy. Which was ironic.

Breakfast was a couple of muesli bars and an apple. The radio was still talking about the football. I wondered if they had been all night.

I had 35 fairly hilly miles to do, but all day to do it in. I was leaving Gloucestershire and would spend most of the day cycling through Herefordshire. Four counties done. Also, I would be visiting allegedly lovely towns. There were reasons to be cheerful. Surely.

I wheeled Scott outside and my host appeared.

"You know," she said, "I should have put you in the other block."

"Oh?"

"Yes. It's much nicer."

"Oh."

She led me into another set of sheds. There was a large room, high-ceilinged, with bunks around the outside and comfy chairs in the middle. There was a fire-place and a telly. It was light and airy, and about a 1000% better than my 'block'.

"I should have put you in here."

"No, no," I said. "Yes," I thought.

But, and this was quite a big but, at least I hadn't been in a tent last night. I had seriously considered camping on this trip. If I had been camping, I'd have had all my wet things squeezed into the tent with me last night; Scott would have been absolutely soaked; and I'd have been loading a wet, heavy tent on to my panniers this morning, together with a sleeping bag and cooking gear. Also, the hostel was seriously cheap. Not much more than the cost of camping. So, cheap and dry. Fine. I said goodbye to my host with a smile on my face.

With the panniers back on the bike and yellow waterproof top on, I emerged out on to the road partway up the hill that led through the gap in the Malvern Hills. It turned out to be half a mile uphill right from the start. I'm not generally a morning sort of person, so this was doubly hard. I stopped several times, using copious tissues. I think my smile had gone.

There was then a mile and a half of continuous downhill, and I was even shattered at the bottom and had to stop. This did not bode well for the day. I limped (if you can limp on a bike) into Ledbury on the 4.3 mile mark.

I chained my bike up next to St Katherine's Hall, which had an amazingly busy Women's Institute market – plants, cakes and so on. Ledbury was buzzing. And all against the background of wonderful black-and-white timber-framed buildings.

The most prominent is Market House, which stands on high legs above the market place below, making – quite literally – a picture-postcard scene. Against white plaster, the black-painted timber frame has a chevron pattern, while other buildings around have square and rectangular shapes.

In a little side alley, Church Lane, black-and-white buildings line each side, their second storeys leaning out above the alley, pulling the eye towards the narrowing church spire at the far end. These 17th century buildings were prefabricated. On the Old Grammar School building, you can still see the Roman numerals to show where the parts fitted. The building is on its third site, so the instructions work.

The best bits of Ledbury's buildings are spectacular. Unfortunately, the 20th century has also struck. A certain well-known chemist-chain has a modern and totally out of place shop-front underneath two stories of timber-framed glory, right by the Market House. It's a mockery. Who in their right minds – whether the builders, the retailers or the council – could possibly have thought it was OK to put a modern shop-front in such an otherwise grand building?

"See this old wood-stuff?"

"Yes."

"Let's have it out."

"Alright."

"Bit o' plastic instead."

"Yes. Good. It'll make it stand out."

"You can't beat plastic."

Please, go to Wells. Look at their market place. Look at Barclays Bank there. Turn the clock back. Please.

I crossed over looking for a different chemist where I could buy more tissues, but couldn't see one. As I was dithering, a couple of schoolgirls giggled. I caught the word 'banana' passing between them. I still had my yellow waterproof top on at this stage – it was damp and chilly, and the panniers had their waterproof covers on as well. Also, unfortunately, yellow.

Scott, smugly: "I think they were saying that you look like a banana."

Me: "Technically, the panniers are part of you."

Silence from Scott.

Me: "So, really, we are a banana."

Silence again. I might have offended him.

We set off for Bromyard, and the route turned out to be constant ups and downs.

At the top of one hill, I glanced up, and I think I was looking at a red kite. Where I live, we have buzzards, kestrels and peregrines, but I had never seen a red kite before. It looked sort of the wrong shape for a buzzard and was too big for a kestrel or a peregrine. I knew that red kites had been re-colonising parts of England from their stronghold in mid Wales, so I stopped to watch.

Red kites were almost driven to extinction by persecution

100 years ago, but conservation and a change of attitude from farmers and landowners has seen the numbers rise from 30 pairs in Wales in the 1970s to 450 pairs now, with the birds spilling over into Shropshire and Herefordshire. There has also been a reintroduction by the RSPB in seven different areas of the UK.

My kite soared gracefully on thermals, not even a flap of its long tapered wings. I leaned on the bike, captivated, until the bird glided gently away, and I had no excuse but to go on. On either side were apple orchards and hop fields. Twenty-foot poles supported cat's cradles of twine, up which green hop plants were curling. Apples for cider, hops for beer. This was good country.

It was 13 miles into Bromyard, constantly up and down, and with a strong wind. There's an almost unfailing rule of cycling that if there is a wind, it's always against you. This one was against me. The last five miles were a struggle, and the last mile more so, as Bromyard came into sight – on a hill.

I finally swayed to a halt in the Market Place and chained Scott up to a tree by The Hop Pole pub. It occurred to me that I had passed other The Hop somethings on the way here, plus all the hop fields. This was Hop City.

I followed signs for the Heritage Centre which I was sure would tell me everything I ever wanted to know about hops. The sign was encouraging: "Newly Re-opened". Excellent.

It was closed.

The rain came on again. I headed back to a café for a fortifying bacon and tomato bap accompanied by huge quantities of tea, and shared wind complaints with two cyclists. If you see what I mean.

Back at the bike, a clock struck quarter past one and I looked up to find a fairly unusual clock on the black-and-pink timber-framed shop belonging to a 'countryside artist'. On the right-hand side of the clock was a four foot high model of an artist, complete with easel, paint brushes, smock and leering expression. On the left-hand side was a four foot high blonde lady with bare legs and arms, and whose torso was only covered by a large fan. The effect of the clock striking the quarter hour was that the lady slowly twirled round, raising her fan to reveal that her torso was also bare. I was tempted to wait and see what happened on the half-hour and the three-quarter-hour, though I suspect the excitement of the hour might have been too much for me.

A sign led me out of Bromyard in the right direction. A novel experience. 'Tenbury 11 miles', it said. Two miles later, another sign said '7 miles'. This was even better. Half a mile later there was another sign: '7½ miles', and another 1½ miles after that: '7 miles'. I was back on track, and now there were old-fashioned stone mile-posts every mile leaving no room for doubt: 'Tenbury 6 – Bromyard 5'. Either that or it was a particularly exciting football match.

I was in Worcestershire now, if only for a few miles. I was clipping the corner, so not counting it in my big twelve counties on the route. It was nice though. The hop fields and orchards were gone, but the country was green, with horses and cows in most of the fields, and the sun came out. I took the yellow covers off the panniers, but kept my jacket on to fend off the wind. I was probably slightly less like a banana.

In Tenbury I had more tea and read about the town really being Tenbury Wells. The name was changed in the 19th century to try to attract the wealthy to come and take the waters here rather than at Bath, Harrogate or Leamington Spa. Pump rooms were built in the wonderfully named 'Chinese Gothic' style. It didn't really work though, and the town never did achieve quite the same status.

Seven miles to go to Ludlow, I worked out, sitting in a tea-shop. I was very tired and it seemed a long way. I debated whether to go and find the Chinese Gothic pump rooms or to press on to Ludlow to be in time to get in to the castle before it closed. On balance it seemed like a good idea to get to Ludlow as early as possible. Wretched cold, I thought. Go away.

The back road to Ludlow wiggles its way up a river valley, but as I passed the Shropshire sign, the road rose. It had just the sort of ups and downs that a fit and healthy cyclist can use to gain plenty of momentum and speed on the downhills, so that a rapid burst of leg-power takes him most of the way up the other side. However, the operative word back there was healthy. I was struggling up each hill and having a rest at the top, standing there breathing heavily in alternating sun and cloud. The road through Greete and Caynham was probably delightful, but I really wanted to be in Ludlow now.

As I climbed one particularly nasty hill, I glanced up. Ahead of me, stationary at the top were a couple of cyclists. A proper "couple". Or at least I assumed they were because he was leaning towards her and kissing her. It was not a peck on the cheek, but, well, there were no tongues.

I put my head down and studied my knees as I inched up the slope, and when I looked ahead of me again (always a good idea on roads) they were both watching me.

I had to say something, and I almost used the words cyclists often use to each other: "Are you going far?" But the image came to me of the man leering and saying, "Oh, yes," then over-toppling into his companion and them falling in a giggling tangle of bikes, arms and legs.

"Nice, er, weather," I said.

"Yes," he said. "Hot," and he grinned.

I reached the A49 straddling the route in front of me, the sun came out all over again and there was Ludlow ahead of me. Downhill. I liked Ludlow.

In fact, I really liked Ludlow. I coasted down into the town where I found the Feathers Hotel. It seemed to have expanded out of its original black-and-white building and taken over half the street. It looked very posh and maybe Bill

Bryson would have said, 'It was expensive but timber-framed.' I wasn't staying there.

I dismounted to walk through a pedestrianised road busy with shoppers and into the market. Stalls of flowers and vegetables and cheeses filled the area, which was surrounded by stately Georgian buildings.

"Scott, this is lovely."

"You're talking to yourself again," he said.

I was just in time for a scoot around the castle before it closed.

The castle feels like an appendage to the town, but originally it was the other way around. The castle was built first and the town grew around it. When William the Bastard, as he was widely known even before he conquered England, needed a means to hold down his rebellious Anglo-Saxons, he came up with a grand scheme. He gave vast stretches of conquered land to his French supporters and told them to make sure they held it. The means to do so was castles.

A Walter de Lacy was given this area and found a

promontory above the rivers, ideal for the purpose. The first castle would have been a mound with a wooden structure on top and a fenced area around the outside: a motte-and-bailey. By the 14th century all that had been swept aside and a vast stone castle built in its place. I walked around its ruins.

It is just ruins unfortunately. The outer wall is still in place, but the stone keep is a shell, and so are the other buildings. Only the size of the castle gives a clue to the power of its previous owners.

It's not with the early Normans that Ludlow is most associated, but the family who dominated the area in the 13th and 14th centuries – the Mortimers. An interesting lot. Mostly called Roger or Edmund. But what they lacked in imagination, they had in ambition.

There was a Roger Mortimer who helped King Edward II's wife, Queen Isabella, seize power from her husband. The two became lovers, and ruled the country together. The King was forced to abdicate in favour of his young son, and Mortimer and the Queen ruled the country together. King Edward was obviously in the way, and Mortimer had him murdered. Strong rumour at the time was that he was killed by having a red-hot poker inserted where the sun doesn't shine, but it seems that Mortimer's enemies may have made that bit up. Either way, when Edward II's son – another Edward – was old enough, he was never going to be happy with the murderer of his father in charge of his country. Mortimer was arrested and executed.

The Mortimers were not finished though and were very close to Richard II (*This royal throne of kings, this scepter'd isle, This earth of majesty, this seat of Mars ... This blessed plot, this earth, this realm, this England*). Thank you, Shakespeare. Richard II was ousted by Henry IV (*Part I*) but by then had named a Mortimer as his heir. As a result another Mortimer descendant, who called Ludlow Castle home, would claim the throne as King Edward IV.

70

When this Edward died, his sons came under the protection of his brother – another Richard. Richard Of York Gave Battle In Vain – that Richard. The one who made himself Richard III and who took the young princes to the tower of London, where they were murdered. (Unless of course you take the opposite view of Richard to that handed us by Shakespeare – which I guessed I would find when I reached Yorkshire in about 10 days time.)

Anyway, the princes in the tower had been brought up in Ludlow Castle, and no doubt played in the rooms of the now ruined buildings I walked through. I always think that ruins are just ruins until you know a story about them. Then your mind goes back and sees life as it was, and the ruins become places of life and movement and – in the case of Ludlow Castle – power.

The castle was closing for the day when I returned to the entrance. Scott was waiting patiently. We cycled gently out to the bed-and-breakfast we were staying in. Scott had a conservatory to spend the night in. I had a warm bed, with a telly, tea-and-coffee-making facilities and fluffy towels. Expensive but with fluffy towels.

I walked back into town to find something to eat. The Feathers looked a bit posh for me from the outside, but the bar menu had a tempting Beef and Ale Pie at a reasonable price, so I settled myself into a comfortable seat and sent a text on my mobile phone to my friend from Ludlow.

'Hi Hugh, fancy a pint of Shropshire Lad and a Beef and Ale Pie in The Feathers?'

Unfortunately, he lives in York now.

'Love to,' he replied.

Captain's log: Day Six
The day's distance: 38.56 miles / 61.70 Km
The journey so far: 200.76 miles / 321.22 Km
Average speed: 10.7 mph / 17.12 Kmph
Maximum speed: 34.5 mph / 55.20 Kmph
Me: mmm, fluffy towels

Day Seven

**Target: 31 miles from Ludlow to Coalport,
via Stokesay Castle, Wenlock Priory and Ironbridge**

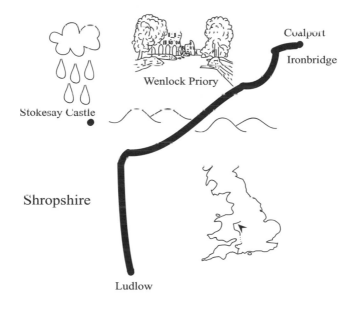

The bed-and-breakfast was complete luxury compared to the previous night. But then, most places would be. The bathroom was in the 'designer-beach-combing' style. The breakfast was big and fried. And the television in the bedroom had a choice of BBC and ITV weather forecasts.

The BBC went for 'grey but dry' while ITV said 'very wet'. Now, I am a 'cup-half-full' sort of guy usually. Besides, it was the BBC. I decided I didn't even need my banana jacket on when I loaded up the panniers. It would be grey but dry and I would cycle into Ludlow town centre again for another look around. I only had 31 miles to do today in grey but dry weather. No problem.

I put the banana jacket on about 100 metres down the road. It was grey, dry and cold.

I decided against the yellow pannier covers for Scott. "Don't worry," I told him. "The BBC says it's going to be dry."

Ludlow was humming. The market was on again and the shops were busy. I pottered down alleyways finding little up-market businesses and well-kept town-houses with the stylish front doors that only the Georgians seem to have mastered. It all looked very prosperous.

I picked up a leaflet for the Ludlow Green Festival starting the following day. The theme was climate change. There would be a carnival with horse-drawn rather than motorised floats, a 'green' fashion show, talks, walks and kite-making. I particularly fancied Walk 6: 'Bronze Age meets Bio-Digester'. I had no idea what it was about but felt sure that Walk 7 must be something like 'Bio-Digester meets Godzilla'.

I definitely liked Ludlow. I certainly felt good about being on a bike.

Only the man begging with a dog and tin-whistle and the man selling The Big Issue suggested that even Ludlow is not immune from real life.

The A49 had a cycle lane as far as my turning. The plan was to take to the country lanes north-west up to Stokesay Castle, a bit out of my way really, then cut across Wenlock Edge eastwards. That was a good plan, except that the BBC dry day seemed to be turning into the ITV wet day. Spots at first, but as I turned off the main road, the rain became harder.

There should have been a lane going off on the left now, parallel with the main road, but with a golf course on either side, there was nothing. Nothing but an increasingly heavy downpour. Ahead of me were some trees and I cycled towards them, cursing the BBC for being wrong and ITV for being right.

"Scott," I said. "You know what this means."

"Banana?"

"Banana."

With Scott's pannier covers in place, I struggled into my waterproof trousers (which thankfully are black and not yellow) and put on my waterproof overshoes (ditto) and we waited in the copse for the shower to stop. It didn't. The 'shower' became a 'prolonged shower'.

As the trees became increasingly sodden, I had two choices – to go back to the main A49 and cycle in what was now a downpour to Stokesay Castle, or to carry on eastwards on the country lane, forget the castle, and try to find a tea-shop.

Castle? What castle?

By the time the bike computer showed ten miles for the day, with constant heavy rain, huge puddles, splashing cars, damp tissues for my nose, and no sign of a café, I was in need of a break. I stopped under a tree to re-fuel – sultanas, nuts, drink – and convinced myself I could make Much Wenlock, which was another ten miles ahead over Wenlock Edge.

It had taken quite a bit to convince myself of that, so when I came to a tea-shop half a mile ahead I took the Scott of the Antarctic view rather than the Scott of the Tea-Shop view, took a deep breath, and ploughed on. I was quite proud of myself until the road started to rise on to Wenlock Edge, when the decision seemed to be more Scott of the Bonkers Decisions.

Then my glasses fell apart.

I'd brought clear plastic glasses – not because I need them to see, but to keep out any rain. At the top of the hill I realised that the nose-bridge was missing – the nose-bridge that prevents the sharp bits of plastic digging into your nose. I could cycle back and look for it, or I could live with rain and muck splashing eyewards, or I could have sharp bits of plastic dig into my nose. The chances of finding the nose-bridge again seemed slim, so I decided to alternate the other options. I did have sunglasses with me, but the day was already pretty dark; I wouldn't see anything with sunglasses on.

I put my clear glasses back on, and ignored the pointy bits digging into my nose.

Wenlock Edge is a long green ridge with views off either side. Rather like the Mendips. Only wetter. It turned out to be another 12 miles to Much Wenlock. So on 22 for the day, I pulled up outside a tea-shop in the village, wet and tired, just as the rain stopped.

It was rather a smart place, with big wooden tables, newspapers to read, and fancy teas and coffees. There were no other customers there at all this Saturday brunch-time, so I happily took over a table for four in the middle and hung my wet waterproofs and damp shirt off chairs. With a cappuccino and a panini, I helped myself to a newspaper to read how England would win the World Cup. I even eased wet feet out of wet trainers under the table. It was wonderful.

So wonderful that time passed without my realising it. People came in and ordered fancy teas and coffees. People came in and ordered lunch. People came in and – when I finally raised my head and looked around – were queuing for a table whilst a cyclist had damp, smelly waterproofs hanging off four different chairs in prime position in the middle of a smart café. I realised that steam and interesting aromas were rising gently from me and decided that perhaps it was time to move on.

Much Wenlock was quaint, and was busying up in the drying day. Weekend tourists were pottering into cafés and antique shops, and into the museum and timber-framed court house. These, I thought, would wait for later on – wet (ITV) weather visits, and I cycled down the road to the Priory for a dry (BBC) visit.

I don't normally pick up one of the audio-guides – the walkie-talkie shaped device where you press buttons to have a commentary as you move around. Often, they go too slow, have too much information, or are not tremendously entertaining. I made an exception, and was pleased I did.

The story was told by 'the last monk at Wenlock Priory'. It had been a 'Cluniac' monastery, founded to rigorously enforce the teachings of St Benedict. Monks' simple and celibate lives were to be entirely devoted to prayer. It had been set up when Kings of England were French, and was a daughter-house of a French monastery. This was not a problem at first, but as France increasingly became the enemy, Wenlock Priory came to be seen as an alien house. Whenever there was a war with France, extra taxes were laid on them, and through the Hundred Years War against the French, that amounted to a massive amount. The Priory built up huge debts, and found that trade was the only way to pay them. Trade took them away from the rigors of monastic life and St Benedict's rules were increasingly forgotten. By the time Henry VIII was looking for a source of more income to fight the French, Wenlock Priory was an all too obvious target. The Prior had, after all, just had sumptuous rooms built for himself. Like Glastonbury and many others, Wenlock Priory was closed. The lead was stripped from the roof to make shot for the French wars, and without the roofs, the building collapsed. Grass grows where the stone flags were walked by the monks.

On the way out I sampled the new English Heritage mead, which was very good. I decided against the mead laced with whisky.

Sounded a bit too good for a cyclist.

When the Priory was closed, the village lost its Court House. The new one they built is still there – an imposing timber-framed first-floor building above what was an open-sided corn market, later enclosed to be a gaol. A council chamber was added to the upper floor a few years afterwards, the inside walls having gorgeously carved and polished wood panelling. Today, there was an exhibition by local artists, and it made a gentle interlude to the day.

I decided on a very quick tour of the museum opposite. Just in and out, then on my way.

"Did you come here specifically to find out about projection machines?"

"Pardon?" I said. I had stepped inside the museum door and was faced by a tall man standing by a large cinema-projection thingy.

"This one has a…"

I think that's when my eyes glazed over.

Except, except, one nugget that stuck. He showed me the film that was threaded through the machine and said, "The sound is on the outside, of course."

"Sorry? The sound?"

It hadn't occurred to me that the film which carries each individual frame of a moving picture also has to carry the sound, and it appears along the outside track of the same piece of film. Now, bet you didn't know that.

I escaped, and can't remember anything about the rest of the museum either. I think my eyes were still glazed.

Back at the door, the man had his back to me, and was greeting a newcomer. "Did you come here…"

I snook out.

It was five miles to Ironbridge over a ridge, but the sun was out, I was warm and my lethargy was gone. My stop in Wenlock had done me good.

The road into the Severn Gorge at Ironbridge was a long, long downhill through woods which dripped atmospherically. I was suddenly at a car park and there was the iron bridge itself.

The bridge has a graceful shape, its iron frame forming a semi-circle supporting a gentle upside-down V of cobbles and iron.

It was busy with tourists photographing the bridge, photographing themselves, photographing themselves photographing the bridge, and so on. I decided to experiment with the timer on the camera and photographed myself by the bridge. Not a bad photo, if you ignore the edge of the bin that the camera was sitting on and the constipated look on my face.

The bridge's innate beauty is only part of the place though. The other part is the history. In the early 18th century, Abraham Darby was the first to make iron on an industrial scale from the burning of coke as a fuel, rather than charcoal. Suddenly, iron could be made in much greater quantities than ever before. This was revolutionary. Over the next century, he and his son and grandson, Abraham Darby II and III – yes, more lack of imagination – made this valley of Coalbrookdale the forefront of a second iron age.

The valley seethed with the new industry, smoke rising and filling every corner, every lung, as iron rails and wheels, steam locomotives and iron boats were all made here and found their way out of the valley along the narrow river below. It was hard to believe looking around at the heritage site now, with children eating ice creams in the sun and old ladies buying bargain cardigans.

The most famous of the Darbys is Abraham III, and that's because he built the bridge. Made from cast iron sections weighing 5 tonnes each, it spans the 100 feet (30 metres) across the Severn. Not big by today's standards, but leading the world in its day. The modern world, you could argue, started right here. I bought an ice cream and astonished myself all over again at how lovely the valley is now.

I cycled on up the road beside the river, peaceful woods all around me, to Coalport China Works. Two huge brick-built kilns curved sensuously up from the valley floor next to a small canal.

I'd been here before. When I was seventeen in the Lower Sixth at school (I can't get used to schools now calling it Year 12), our school encouraged us to go off on working weeks. Something environmental, or in my case archaeo-logical. We came here to dig the rubble out of one of these giant kilns so that eventually they could be opened to the public. We shovelled and dug and wheelbarrowed during the day, and at night we went on illicit trips to the pub.

The China Works are open to the public now, part of the tremendous Ironbridge Gorge Museum Trust, which includes nine different museums.

The hostel turned out to be part of the original China Works factory buildings, but has been magically transformed inside. Everything is new and splendid, and there are even single rooms. There was also a kitchen, a laundry with a washing machine (hooray), a large warm drying room, hot showers, a games room, a TV lounge, internet access and even a restaurant. This was perfect. Well, nearly. The transformation has left the internal walls a little thin, and running children were a touch noisy that night. But even so, this must be what the YHA is trying to turn itself into. This they must see as the future.

The YHA has a problem (above and beyond the financial one). As I was finding, the main users of youth hostels are not youths any more. They've become middle-age and grey-haired. Children come in school parties, but the Youth Hostel Association needs to get them to come back when they are young adults, or the YHA becomes old (the OHA) and eventually dies (the DHA).

The lady at reception suggested I leave Scott in the warm

drying room by the front door, which went down very well with Scott, and I booked a meal in the restaurant.

I went to the kitchen to make myself a (free) coffee and found a man of roughly my age peeling considerable numbers of potatoes. I'll call him Philip. He was here with his four daughters. One of them was at the same university as my oldest daughter. The youngest was slightly younger than my youngest. He looked a capable man, standing there peeling spuds for five, and his clipped accent and bearing suggested a military career. A younger daughter bounced in smiling and chatting, and I said I'd see him later.

I made my way to the restaurant, and found I was the only one eating in a big dining area.

Afterwards, I took another (free) coffee to the TV room, where I found Philip drinking a beer. He was daughter-free and we got to talking again. He asked me about my journey, but was, well, preoccupied. I understood when he told me why. This was a family weekend to try to decide how they would move on after the girls' mother had left them the previous year.

"Oh," I said, "I'm sorry."

He was hurt and perplexed. I don't know if he was right to feel those things, but that's what he was. Suddenly my own journey seemed insignificant. His was much harder. We talked for a long time, until four pretty daughters joined him.

"Daddy, are you drunk?" one said.

"No, I'm just telling this gentleman here about your mother."

"Oh, Daddy," she said indulgently. "What's on telly?" Her fingers found the remote and our talk ended, the family milling around happily.

"Good night," I said to Philip. "And good luck."

"See you in the morning," he said.

82

Captain's log: Day Seven
The day's distance: 30.42 miles / 48.67 Km
The journey so far: 231.18 miles / 369.89 Km
Average speed: 11.0 mph / 17.6 Kmph
Maximum speed: 34.5 mph / 55.2 Kmph
Me: both depressed and heartened by people, all at the
same time

Day Eight

**Target: 46 miles from Coalport to Oakamoor in the
Staffordshire Moorlands, via Shifnal, Gnossal,
Great Bridgeford and Stone**

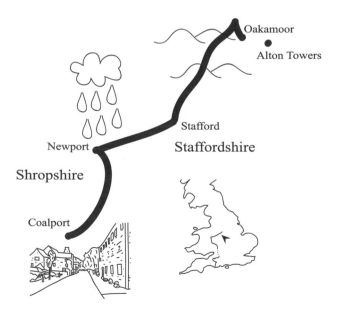

The EXTRA-STRONGS were all gone.

This was, of course, pretty disastrous. Worse was that the YHA man looked up the weather on the internet and said it was going to rain.

I had a couple of cold-relief tablets, (free) coffee from the kitchen and a couple of muesli bars. There was no sign of Philip and his family. I didn't know if they had got up at an early military hour and gone, or if the girls were having a lie in. I suspected that Philip was now outranked. So I took a page from my notebook and left a message for my friend propped on the reception desk.

To Philip.
Safe journey.
Mike

I don't know if he got it, and if he did, whether he understood which of his journeys I meant.

I put on my jacket, but not all the waterproof kit – it wasn't raining just yet – and wheeled Scott out of the drying room to lean him against the wall. A spot of rain landed on my face.

"Is this going to be one of those days?" he said.

"No."

"It was warm and dry in there."

"This is just a drying-up shower," I said. "It won't last."

"Pull the other one."

A mile up the wooded floor of the valley, my road turned left. Up and out of the valley. It was very, very steep, and the rain was increasing now. I had to stop to get my breath a good number of times. At the top it had to be full waterproofs and pannier covers. It was the banana again.

As soon as the road levelled out at the top, it was as if I was in a different country. The woods were gone. The remains of a great industrial past were gone. Instead I was in arable land – some fields ready for planting, others with young green wheat growing through. I cycled into Shifnal and found a petrol station where I was able to re-stock on tissues and EXTRA-STRONGS, and to have a chocolate bar for some instant energy.

I had hoped to visit Boscobel House, just outside Shifnal, site of The Royal Oak. Not a pub, but a tree.

The final battle of the English Civil War – the battle of Worcester in 1651 – had seen a young King Charles II fleeing the parliamentarian forces to a Catholic home at Boscobel House. His father, Charles I, had been beheaded and the monarchy had been abolished; families had been divided, fathers fighting sons, brothers fighting brothers; there had been massacres of both sides in a war entwining parliament versus king, and hard-line Protestants versus bishop-led church and Catholicism. This was not a jolly roundheads versus cavaliers re-enactment. It was as bloody and awful as many another civil war in our own living memory. So if Charles were found, he was a dead man.

In the grounds of Boscobel House, Charles hid in an oak tree from the pursuing troops, and once they had gone, hid in the house before he escaped to France. England might have remained a Republic to this day had not the lords and people of England become thoroughly fed up with the dominance of the army and the religious bigotry that went with the Protectorate of England under Oliver Cromwell.

When Cromwell died, Charles II was invited back – on terms. And England started the road that would lead eventually to parliamentary democracy, a figurehead monarchy, and pubs throughout the land being named The Royal Oak. I'd drink to that, if I could.

From under the canopy of the petrol station, the rain didn't look too bad really. The trouble was, today was a long day. It was supposed to be 46 miles, but previous experience suggested it would be more if I stuck with my country lanes meandering through Shropshire and Staffordshire. Also, country lanes often didn't have places to stop to get warm and dry(-ish). I came to a decision. I would not stand under an oak tree communing with Charles II's spirit. Nor would I meander through lanes. No, today I would stick to A-roads and go through towns. It was Sunday morning, for heaven's sake. The roads would be quiet. It would probably shorten the journey.

By the time I was approaching Newport, I was cold and wet and a little dispirited. My A-road didn't actually go into Newport. There was a by-pass. But I felt I deserved some dryness. A café was needed. Or a pub. Perhaps there would be a Royal Oak. Anything.

I'd forgotten, unfortunately, that it was Sunday morning. Newport is closed on a Sunday morning. Every single café, pub or bar was closed. Why? Surely there's demand for something at 10 o'clock on a wet Sunday? No? I even contemplated going to a church. They often have coffee and biscuits after a service. They'd probably welcome me as a man on a pilgrimage.

I got to speculating which variety of church would have the best biscuits. Methodists would probably be Rich Tea. Church of England might be Digestive. Catholic could be Bourbon. That would be good. I was just wondering which would be Chocolate Hobnobs when I noticed that a pub called The Barley had a sandwich board outside saying 'Open All Day for Good Food'. In triumph I leaned Scott against the wall, stood under the canopy of the door and took off my helmet. I pulled at the door. Nothing. It was very firmly closed.

This was so depressing, and what was more depressing was that I realised that my Lifa top under my waterproof jacket was feeling very wet. Either my jacket was leaking or the rain was getting down my neck. It didn't seem a good idea to be cycling in pouring rain with Man-Flu and a wet shirt on. Yet there was nowhere to change. I looked around. Nothing. So there was no choice really. I fished out two dry shirts (a thin one and a thick one), stripped off my jacket and my Lifa top down to my goose-pimpled skin, and put on two dry layers. At least if my jacket was leaking, it would take longer to get through to the skin. I also tightened the neck of my jacket to a just-breathing closeness to my throat. Please, I thought, stay dry.

Now I had to go on. I needed movement to warm me up again.

Forget, I thought, Gnossal and Great Bridgeford and all those little villages. I changed the route arbitrarily and completely, and headed towards Stafford on the main A-road. On an A-road there would surely be somewhere to stop and get dry.

I passed The Navigation.

No.

The Cyclists' Rest.

No.

The Sprocket and Cycle-Clip.

No.

The Come And Get Dried And Have Something To Eat.

No.

All the while the road undulated, the rain came down, lorries and cars steamed past, and I half hated those fluttering little England flags and half wished I had one on the back of the bike. The backdraft from a lorry swished me sideways and then a white van came much too close as it passed.

"I've got your number," I shouted, but I suspect my threats went unheeded.

I was all the way to Stafford before there was anywhere to stop.

The 'anywhere', when it came, was Tescos. 28 miles of rain and traffic and Man-Flu, and the sight of an almighty-great Tescos led me to thank the Lord for the Sunday trading laws that allowed it to be open.

The shop (shop?) – the megastore had a somewhat larger

canopy than the one outside The Barley, and I chained Scott there. I must admit to a little reticence about leaving him. Not that I wanted to take him inside, but that this felt much less secure than leaving him, say, outside a ruined abbey, or a castle. Then I noticed the security camera above my head and felt better about it.

I took my last dry shirt out of a pannier and dripped my way past the fresh fruit towards the escalators. These took me to the restaurant where I selected a table as far away from the counter as possible. That meant one that looked down on assembled Sunday-shoppers below. Waterproof jacket, trousers and over-shoes were soon hanging from chairs and I realised that my twin shirts were dry. The wetness must have come in at the neck. My waterproof jacket was waterproof. On balance, that was good news.

Internal heat came from a Big Brunch while reading that England were still going to win the World Cup. Or might if the Football Correspondent's own team and tactics were selected.

Stafford, it occurred to me, must be in Staffordshire. County number seven. Six down out of the twelve. Not half way in terms of miles. Not by a long way, but six counties felt good.

I sat there for a long time. Long enough for medium-sized puddles to have formed under chairs. It was no good getting too comfortable though. I reassessed my route and the likely mileage. If I had done 28 miles, I still had about another 20-odd to do, and there would now be some fairly significant hills. I thought about the rain, I thought about the 20-odd miles, I thought about the hills, and I put my third shirt on over the other two. Then the waterproof jacket.

Astonishingly, it seemed to have been dry outside while I had been in Tescos. As soon as I set off, though, a light drizzle appeared.

"Balderdash," I said. Or something like that. I think it

started with a B anyway.

Cycling through Stafford wasn't too bad. There were useful little cycle lanes at junctions and roundabouts, and I even found the road towards Cheadle without getting lost. I also had a Tescos Big Brunch inside me for sustenance.

The new-found energy turned out to be fairly short-lived as the hills started properly. A big uphill would be followed by a shorter downhill. I was climbing, and pretty soon I was shattered. At least it was only drizzling still.

At Draycott another big hill loomed, as did a pub at its base.

"I need the energy," I said to Scott.

I squeezed three cups of tea out of a tea-pot, and answered queries from the landlord about my destination.

"Berwick-upon-Tweed. But not today. I'm staying at Oakamoor YHA tonight."

As I left, into returned rain, a waitress waved me off. "Good luck," she said.

I looked at the hill. I might need it. It wasn't the worst hill though. It was the hill out of Cheadle that was the monster, or felt it after far too many miles.

At least the road was now signposted 'Oakamoor'. Just over this ridge, I said to myself, and Oakamoor is at the bottom of the next valley. Even so, there were a number of 'breathing stops' on the way up. Not for long though. Even with my three shirts and waterproof, if I stopped for more than a few minutes I was getting very cold.

I think it was at this point that I first started to wonder how it was that you got pneumonia. Wasn't it something to do with getting wet and cold when you already had a bug of some sort?

There was a very steep descent through woods on the other side of the ridge. Oakamoor was a long way down. My brakes didn't feel too good. Didn't really feel that they were slowing me down as much as I would have liked.

"Come on, Scott. Don't do this."

"You don't appreciate what I've been through."

"What?!"

"When did you last clean me and see to my brakes?"

"Well…"

Oakamoor on a wet Sunday late-afternoon was very quiet. There were only a few houses and a couple of hostelries, and I slithered to a halt amongst them. I thought a pub might be nice later. I'd potter back from the Youth Hostel.

A YHA sign took me off to the right up a gently rising lane. The lane rose a bit more, and a bit more. Finally it got towards proper steepness. A man was walking down.

I stopped, brakes on to stop me rolling backwards.

"Is there a Youth Hostel up there?" I asked.

"Um. I think so."

Not useful. Not encouraging.

There were various houses dotted amongst the woods, but none of them had a YHA sign.

Then there was a couple walking down.

"Is there a Youth Hostel up there?" I asked.

"Yes."

"Is it far?"

"Well, you keep on going up. Then you take the left fork. Then you go up again until you get to the top of the ridge."

"The top of the ridge?"

"Yes."

"I've just come from the top of the ridge."

"Ah. Well, then you follow the lane for about a half a mile, and you're there."

All thoughts of pottering back down to the pub disappeared.

I fought my way up the hill (with yet more 'breathing stops') and found myself back on the ridge. The rain stopped as I got there, and a gap appeared in the clouds. The sun even came out. There were fields at the top, and I cycled along

farm lanes until, finally, the hostel came into sight set roman-
tically amongst oak woods, with a view across to the topmost
tower of the actual castle at Alton Towers a few miles away.
The rumour of noisy fun from the rides found its way
through the trees. It was 5 o'clock and my bike computer
said 49.9 miles. I was a bit tired really.

The YHA man was in his own little hut. He was waiting
to let me in, he said. I was the only one staying, not even
him, so he'd give me a key, sell me any food that I wanted,
and see me again in the morning.

"Right," I said. "Just me then."

I looked in at the hostel, sitting all by itself surrounded by
woods at the top of a ridge in the middle of nowhere. More
black clouds cut out the sun; thunder rolled across; the last
human left me, and I thought of the horror film recently
released: 'The Hostel'.

Just me, then.

There was no telly, and the radio didn't work, so it was
very quiet. I wheeled Scott into the lounge in case he was
scared and carried my panniers through to choose which
bunkroom I would have. They had names. Like 'Oblivion'
and 'Nemesis'. (Really they did).

As another roll of thunder came across, I put my bags
down in Nemesis.

Captain's log: Day Eight
The day's distance: 49.90 miles / 79.84 Km
The journey so far: 281.08 miles / 449.73 Km
Average speed: 11.0 mph / 17.6 Kmph
Maximum speed: 33.0 mph / 52.8 Kmph
Me: cleaning Scott's chain and brakes on newspapers
spread across the floor of the hostel, while thunder
pounded outside.

And whistling.

Day Nine

**Target: 38 miles from Oakamoor to Hathersage,
via Hartington and Bakewell**

I was not ritually sacrificed during the night. I'm glad about that really.

In fact, when I woke up and looked out the window, it wasn't even raining. I had a bit of a spring in my step as I went through to the lounge.

"Morning, Scott," I said, though the voice was croakier than I expected. "How's the chain this morning? Squeaky clean?"

"Good, thank you," he said. "How was Nemesis?"

"Better than Oblivion, I think."

There was a squirrel on the grass outside the window and I watched him from the quiet of the hostel as I had breakfast. It was misty and murky outside. As I ate, a few raindrops hit the window. In just a few minutes the morning became darker, and the drops bigger.

I put all my things together, tissues stowed in all sorts of reachable places, and said to Scott in my best glass-half-full voice, "We'll wait. It can't do this all morning." It still sounded croaky.

The YHA man arrived in his car and ran across to the hostel in the rain.

"Bit wet," he said.

"Just a bit. Have you seen a forecast?"

"Yes. It's going to do this all morning."

Scott just looked at me from his corner.

Outside, the rain was heaving down. I blew my nose. "I might hold on a bit if that's OK?"

"Yes, that's fine. I'm waiting for the guy coming to service the fire-extinguishers."

I came to a firm decision about my planned route for the day. I wasn't going to do it. I had been going to cycle over two fairly serious ridges – the highest on my ride so far – on country lanes and off-road cycle ways, seeing the best of the Peak District. County number eight: Derbyshire. I'd been really looking forward to it. There would be sun, and hills, and views, and… No, in this rain with continuing Man-Flu, I needed towns to stop in every now and then, and I didn't need whacking great hills in pouring rain. The plan went out the window, to somewhere where the squirrel was cavorting. I would cycle around the hills via Ashbourne and Matlock. It was further and would involve A-roads, but I was less likely to end up in an ambulance with some combination of hypothermia, pneumonia, diphtheria and trench foot.

The servicing of the fire extinguishers was too speedy if you ask me. I think he needed to take much longer over them. A couple of hours perhaps. But no, he was done in about ten minutes, and the YHA man gave me a sort of look which said, 'Push off then, wimp,' while his voice said, "No rush."

He also said, "The weather forecaster was saying that the rainfall this May has been 143% of the usual May rainfall."

"Oh," I said.

"Yes. Something like the fourth wettest May ever."

"Oh," I said.

"And that's so far. Going to be very wet today."

"Ohooooooooh," I howled.

I didn't actually howl, but it seemed like a good idea. Scott was looking at me again.

The rain eased a touch, and I had no choice really. I put on the full banana works and set off. As I did so, the sun came out. I was really hot in my full waterproofs.

The forest up on the ridge was very pretty, and I took my time on the ups and downs, before that great long descent into Oakamoor again.

Hello, Oakamoor again.

It was a mix of sun and mist down in the valley, and Oakamoor was a pleasant little place, not looking too much like the home of the hard-wiring of the world.

When Morse Code was carrying news and business information across countries and continents in the middle of the 19th century, it was using copper wire made right here.

I stopped on the bridge and looked around me. Quiet houses were set amongst the oak woods along the valley sides. The factory site that had produced sixty tons of cable to cross the Atlantic in 1857 was entirely gone, landscaped away.

The residents have been left with an enchanting wooded valley, only marred by traffic headed the same way as I was. Just along the road was Alton Towers.

I was definitely over-warm as the road took me to the gates. There were countless coaches going in. Thousands of people. Beyond the entrance, my road ran parallel to their access road for a while. I couldn't see anybody, but I could hear them. I was just starting to think what a nice day they'd be having, when the rain started again.

Heavily.

Very heavily.

The shelter of a couple of already very wet trees was not really shelter at all. I decided I would wait out the worst and practised standing as straight and thinly as possible so that the raindrops would have less of a target. It didn't really work. I decided not to do that any more.

The rain got harder. OK, another plan. There were houses up ahead. I would ask them if I could stand in a porch and they might offer me tea and biscuits. Only, they might have seen me practising standing as straight as possible for ten minutes just down the road. They might just consider me unbalanced. I suppose I could get them to talk to Scott and he'd tell them I'm OK really, once you got to know me.

The rain got harder again. OK, another plan. To hell with it, I would just cycle until I got to a town, where I would find a café and get out of soaking wet clothes.

I cycled on, the rain cold on my face and running down my neck. I was vaguely aware that somewhere beyond my bleared vision, there were bluebells lining the hedgerow, and that in other conditions, this was probably a nice place to be cycling. My waterproof trousers seemed conspicuously unwaterproof, but then my reason for buying this particular brand had been cheapness and lightness rather than waterproofness. I think I was in a glass-half-full mood when I bought them. Increasingly I was getting into a glass-half-empty mood as the rain went on and on. My nose was becoming a small fountain and I developed an intermittent cough. I got to thinking about pneumonia again.

The rain did stop once or twice, but when I was about a mile from Ashbourne, heavy rain turned into a torrential tropical downpour. Though without the tropical heat. A bus shelter came up on the left. The shelter had glass sides, and before long I had a small herd of cows standing behind me, brown eyes watching, bemused. Then I had a bus in front of me, the driver looking at me and looking at the bike. Also bemused. He whooshed the door closed and was gone, so I don't know what colour his eyes were.

"So," Scott said, "have you solved the Meaning of Mid-Life yet?"

"How do you expect me to solve the Meaning of Mid-Life when I have rampant Man-Flu?"

"I believe there was an American President who couldn't walk and chew gum at the same time."

"There might have been."

"Is that you then?"

"Yes. No. Maybe," I said in a Man-Flu-y sort of way.

"I will make no comment about the ability of a man to multi-task."

"That," I said, "would be wise."

After half an hour I was getting too cold waiting for the rain to stop. I wondered what pleurisy was. I'd heard of that as well. Also something to do with doing daft wet things when you've got Man-Flu. I sorted a new load of tissues from the box in the pannier, and distributed them to the nose-reachable parts of me, then set off again.

At some point I must have crossed from Staffordshire into Derbyshire, and I did wonder whether I should be looking out for the North-South Divide. Was it something I would fall in to, or bump against? And if so where? Derbyshire seemed a reasonable guess. I would look out for it.

In a café in Ashbourne I did my usual of hanging wet items of clothing from a variety of chairs, and changed my shirt in the toilets.

"Can I get food?" I asked a disinterested man behind the counter.

"Not for half an hour."

"But I can get coffee and read your newspapers in the warm for half an hour and then order food."

"Er, yes."

"One coffee, please."

The rain stopped and out of the window, Ashbourne was bathed in sunshine. Oh balderdash, I said, and drank my coffee and read my paper. England, apparently, could still win the World Cup, but only if they used an entirely different team to the one I'd read could win the World Cup in another paper.

"Cycling?" the lone man on the table next to me asked, observantly.

"Yes," I said, monosyllabically.

"Did you see we've had 143% of the usual rain in May?"

"Yes."

"Mm. Bit wet for cycling."

"Yes," I said. I wasn't feeling very well.

I got my maps out to look at the new route. To my consternation all the hard work that morning seemed only to have gained me twelve miles. It was lunch time already, on a day I was meant to be doing 38 miles. I couldn't believe it and checked it again. Twelve. T.W.E.L.V.E. This was not good news, and probably meant I had about 28 to do that afternoon. T.W.E.N - oh, you know what I mean.

The B-road led me out of Ashbourne gently uphill for a long time in a light drizzle. This was definitely Peak District now, with hard stone houses and farms sprinkled across a green countryside. The road stayed on the ridge for some way and gave me a dramatic view towards the Carsington Water Reservoir. In sunshine, it would probably be lovely down there. Past signs for The Carsington Water Visitor Centre, The Middleton Top Visitor Centre and The Stone Centre – this was tourist country now, and finally the road dropped into Cromford.

From here there was no choice about the route. It was going to be the A6(T) through Matlock Bath and Matlock. This was going to be busy.

The road started to climb and as it did, black clouds started emptying buckets of water directly over my head. Cars, lorries and buses threw more water at me from the side. And my tyres bounced through pot-holes and puddles, splashing and spraying me from underneath. I ground my way up the hill from Cromford towards Matlock Bath and thought of cricket. As you do. When I was about seventeen, I spent a couple of weeks painting walls during the shut-down of the Avon Rubber Company in Bradford on Avon. What I remember most was listening to Radio 4's cricket commentary. The best bits were the breaks for rain.

"Well, Blowers," one would say. (I think cricket people are all Blowers or Tuffers or Aggers or Whatevers.) "What do you think of the fruit cake sent in by Mrs Oojamaflip from Margate?"

"Moist, Buffers. Moist."

It was classic stuff.

I too was moist.

Cromford, like Ironbridge, is one of the birthplaces of the Industrial Revolution. Not for iron and coal, but for cotton. I cycled painfully past 'Sir Richard Arkwright's Mill', which is now part of the Derwent Valley World Heritage Site.

Arkwright was the youngest of 13 children of a poor family. By the time of his death, he had become Sir Richard, High Sheriff of Derbyshire.

In the 1770s – just as the Darbys were working in Coalbrookdale – Arkwright developed the water-powered cotton mill, which helped revolutionise the textiles industry. Where before, skilled workers plied their trade from home, now workers were brought in to work in the new manufactories. From now, the dales of Derbyshire, Yorkshire and Lancashire would become the centres of the cotton and wool industries. Great mill buildings would line the rivers, with rows of terraced houses for the workers. If they were lucky, a good owner (like Arkwright) might build a school and a chapel. Either way, the workers would have long hours in highly unpleasant working conditions.

Iron in Coalbrookdale, cotton in Cromford, this was the new England, the start of modern England. It didn't look like a World Heritage Site in the rain.

I started compiling a Top 10 of overtaking vehicles. Older women drivers with permed hair would be top. They were good, taking a nice wide loop around me. White vans would be bottom.

I stopped in Matlock Bath. The Mining Museum incongruously occupies the grand peach-and-pink-painted Pavilion, where 'the former dance floor has been renovated and converted to provide a setting for the relics of the Peak District's oldest industry. Crawl and climb through a maze of twisted tunnels and shafts to feel for yourself the cramped conditions of a Derbyshire lead miner.' It also sold tea in the old foyer, from where I could watch the rain outside. I had done 24 miles.

I bought postcards and dutifully wrote one to Maggie and the well-dressers of Dorset. I added a PS, "I should stay in Dorset. It's too wet in Derbyshire." I wrote more postcards to friends and family, and on each of them dripped rain which smudged the handwriting. Later, I was asked if the smudges were my tears. "No," I said. "Well, mostly not."

I told the owners I was going to Hathersage, and the lady cyclist amongst them advised me to stick to the main road until the turn off for Chatsworth. I should also stop in Calver at the outdoor-shop's café for tea and a bun. I would, I thought. It was something to aim for. I needed something to aim for.

Along the A6(T) beyond Matlock I placed lorries pretty low on my Top 10. And estate cars. Especially that green one.

I was pleased to turn off towards Chatsworth. As I did so, the rain stopped, but the wind got up. I was cycling north, and that was where the wind was coming from.

The road rose until I suddenly had a view of one of the most palatial of stately homes: Chatsworth House. It seemed a good idea to stop and look at it for a few minutes.

That, at any rate, was what my heaving chest was telling me.

The house still belongs to the Duke of Devonshire, whose ancestor, the first Duke, built it in the classical style at the end of the 17th century. It was an enormous pile, and was simply majestic, its golden stone walls perfectly balanced in the valley below.

It's astonishing to think of the vast wealth that went in to the building of the house and the filling of it with so many paintings that 'England's Thousand Best Houses' called it 'the National Gallery of the North'. So where did the money come from? It might be something to do with the 55 square miles of land across Derbyshire and Staffordshire still owned by the estate, as well as property in London. The Sunday Times Richlist for the previous year had the Duke as the 129th richest person in Britain, somehow down from 104th the previous year despite his wealth increasing by £20 million. Just the £500 million now, they estimated.

It had been part of my plan to go through Eyam, pronounced Eem. The 'plague village'. Plague is one of those words that, merely whispered, has historically brought fear and loathing in its wake. Other words include the black death, leprosy and Man-Flu.

The year 1665 was called the annus mirabilis, the Year of Wonders, with those wonders including a war, the Great Fire of London, and the plague. Some 'Wonders'. Makes you think something must have been lost in translation.

Eyam, a tiny lead-mining community, must have seemed immune from the terrible catastrophes in places like London. Until the first deaths came. They were terrible deaths, with painful sores breaking out on the body, intense fever, and almost no hope of survival.

Nobody knew the cause, but it seemed that somehow the infection could be carried. Which is why the good people of Eyam voluntarily decided to cut themselves off from the world so as not to infect neighbouring villages. They paid a terrible price. Two thirds of the inhabitants died.

With my Man-Flu, perhaps it's a good job I didn't go to Eyam.

I did, though, have tea and a bun in Calver, sneaking in just before they closed, and they were jolly people. It was good to chat with them and take my mind off the last five miles to Hathersage Youth Hostel against the wind.

It turned out to be a hilly five miles. Thankfully, the YHA had omitted to site this particular hostel at the top of an enormous hill, which I had been fully expecting.

Even so.

Even so, I wasn't sure if I could do another day like today. I was totally exhausted. The weather and my cold just seemed to come together at the moment I arrived. I was somewhere near the northern edge of Derbyshire, having surely survived the North-South Divide. But I wasn't feeling at all well.

I sent a text to Hugh, who lives in York but works in Barnsley.

"Hugh, not feeling too good. If I need rescuing, could you help?"

"Scott Tracey to the rescue," he replied.

I looked at my own Scott. "What do you think? Do I go on?"

My Scott, unusually, said nothing.

I was to share a dormitory in the annex with two others. One was a smallish man with neat dark hair and worried eyes. The other, a big guy with a big beard and a big Australian accent, said, "Hi. Mick."

"No, Mike," I replied, shaking a big Australian hand.

The two men looked at each other, and the Ozzie accent said with a smile, "You're Mike? I'm Mick. And he's Michael."

"Mike, Mick and Michael?"

"Looks like it."

Michael was a postman using a walking week to sort his mind out after family and friend tragedies. I asked him if he had read 'The Missing Postman', a book I love. "You should read it," I said. "It's good. It's funny."

Ozzie Mick was from Sydney, but working for the YHA in Ambleside. He parked his bike next to Scott in the bike-shed.

"Where are you cycling to?" I asked.

"Chatsworth. And you?"

"Well, I'm on a long-distance bike ride. To Berwick. From Dorset."

"Hey, that's great."

"Erm, the only thing is, I'm not feeling good. I'm, er, not sure if I can go on."

His head cocked on one side. "You'll be fine. "

"Actually, I'm not sure about that," I said.

I didn't feel the way I had at Bradford on Avon. That was a cold that I had hoped to shake off. I never had. I had cycled for five long days since then, through astonishingly bad weather. Now my chest felt tight and my breathing was laboured, even when I wasn't cycling uphill. I felt drained. Totally, totally drained.

I phoned home, or tried to. The only signal from my mobile phone was a variable one when I stood in the front garden on a drain cover, held the phone a foot above my head, and hopped.

I told Claire I might have to stop.

"I don't want you to be really ill," she said.

"No. Neither do I."

I didn't mention pneumonia.

Back inside, Mick said, "Sleep on it."

I tried to, but I was so full of cold that I could hardly breathe. Big Mick snored, and they were big Ozzie snores.

Captain's log: Day Nine
The day's distance: 42.83 miles / 68.53 Km
The journey so far: 323.91 miles / 518.26 Km
Average speed: 10.1 mph / 16.08 Kmph
Maximum speed: 36.0 mph / 57.6.8 Kmph
The dormitory: Poor Michael. I suspect when I did sleep, I rivalled Big Mick. Dolby Surround-Sound Snoring.

Day Ten

**Target: 48 miles from Hathersage to Mankinholes,
via Holmfirth, Slaithwaite and Hebden Bridge**

● Hathersage

Derbyshire

As soon as I woke, I knew I had to stop. It didn't matter that the sky was Wedgewood Blue only gently touched by little puffy clouds. I felt rotten.

I had booked a full breakfast to set me up for a big cycling day. Mick and Michael were already at the table.

"What are you going to do?" Mick asked.

"I can't do it. I feel wrecked."

"You're stopping?"

"Yes. But just for a while. I'm going to do it. I just have to have a break to get better."

The table was set for four, and a young woman sat down with us. She was twenty-something with smiley eyes and wasn't quite the usual occupant of the youth hostels I'd stayed in. "Hi," she said, "I'm Alice."

"Mick, Michael and Mike," Mick said, and she smiled for some reason.

Alice was starting a new job in Sheffield, and had stayed here so as to go house-hunting. My story came out. I was on my way north, but had to stop. I'd be finding my way out of Hathersage.

"I'll give you a lift," she said.

"What? Really?"

"Sure. I've a couple of houses to look at but that's it today. Where do you want to go?"

I could hardly believe it.

"Well, somewhere towards Barnsley would be good."

"I could take you to Penistone. That's a nice place to wait."

I was, I think, sickeningly grateful.

In fact I was all the more astonished when I went to retrieve Scott and found her sorting her car out. She'd just bought it. Two days ago. It was a low silver sporty thing. Pristine clean. She had just offered to have my dirty oily bike in it, and here she was putting the back seats flat and stretching her towel across the floor for the bike to lie on.

It was funny, I had never heard Scott purring before.

"I'm just going to look at a house down the road," she said. "I'll be back soon."

I gazed at the silver car and the clean blue fluffy towel, and then at Scott. Scott really was absolutely filthy. Grime caked everything. The chain was black and nasty from adding oil to the grime each day.

It didn't seem entirely gentlemanly to put all that on Alice's towel, so I folded her towel and found mine in my panniers. Actually, it's not mine. I was borrowing my daughter's travel towel, gallant survivor of Thailand, Australia and New Zealand. Sorry, Lisa.

I scraped as much mud off Scott as I could and took the wheels off. It looked touch-and-go as to whether it would fit into the back of a sports car. As gently as possible, I lowered the frame into the car. At the last moment, my hand slipped and the frame dropped on to Lisa's towel. The chain left a thick black oily mark on the towel, and dried mud spattered down.

"Ah," I said.

"Oops," Scott said.

Sorry, Lisa.

Panniers and wheels sat on top, and the boot just about closed.

The sun was warm now. I could tell that on my skin, but I felt cold, and sat down in a doorway to exchange texts with Hugh. Penistone at 4pm would be fine. Scott Tracey to the rescue. Thunderbirds are go!

I went around to the front garden to stand on the drain cover, hold the phone above my head and hop.

Through the interference, Claire heard something like this, "not... well... York... Hugh... tomorrow"

Claire phoned me back.

"...well ...could ...pick...please"

I sent her a text message instead.

The route Alice drove me was not very different to the one I had been going to cycle, because she was going to look at a house to let in Low Bradfield, one of the little villages in the hills above Sheffield. As the road went precipitously up and down, there was the odd glimpse off to the east to the city down below us. I had definitely crossed the North-South Divide if I was looking down on steel city. I must have crossed another border somewhere as well. I was no longer in the Derbyshire Peak District. I was in Yorkshire.

In fact we were amazingly close to Sheffield, given that we were so high and otherwise so remote. The villages were tiny and pretty, with country inns and duck ponds, but the house Alice looked at was only half-renovated. She wasn't sure.

"Did the guy look like someone who would finish it off?" I said.

"Mm, well, maybe not."

She told me about her attempts to buy and now to lease somewhere, and about moving from the south to a new job and a new life in Sheffield.

It was lunch time. "Can I buy you lunch by way of thanks for the lift?" I asked.

"I could do with a cold drink."

We stopped at a pub next to Langsett Reservoir, and the sun shone on the To Let board of a cottage round the back. The estate agent responded to Alice's call and twenty minutes later, he was setting off the burglar alarm without knowing the combination to switch it off.

"I've never done that before."

He phoned his office in a small panic.

Alice said to me, "Do you want to look round?"

"Do you want me to?"

"Um, yes, if you don't mind."

What a shame that she was house-hunting by herself. Big decisions are so much easier if you've a friend to talk to them about.

In the living room of the expensively renovated cottage, the agent looked me up and down.

"I'm a friend," I said.

After he'd left, we retreated to the pub and Alice said, "What do you think?"

I mulled it over. "I think it'd be great," I said, "if you're happy with your own company. Langsett's very pretty and the cottage is beautiful. But perhaps you'd be more likely to go out with work colleagues and meet people if you were in Sheffield itself?"

She drove me on to Penistone and dropped me at a bench in the sun next to the church, and I was again pathetically grateful for my rescue. I think she was also glad to have had company.

"Thanks for the little adventure," she said.

I left Scott chained to a bench by the church in Penistone and went off to buy a sandwich. When I came back to the bench to eat it, an elderly lady was sitting there with her shopping bag. She'd have been top of my Top 10 overtakers list if she wasn't waiting for the bus.

"You're lucky I didn't cycle off on your bike," she said, and I had a smile from her. I think it might have been some while since she'd been able to sit on a bike saddle.

She was from Rochdale in Lancashire. Enemy territory, I said, for living here in Yorkshire.

We talked about 'the war', as you do, sitting in the sun with someone you've never met before. The second world war, that is.

She recalled the American soldiers teaching her to jitter-bug. "They were so full of life," she said. "So full of confidence."

"I bet the English lads weren't so keen on them."

"They weren't here. My father told some of the Americans he'd take them to a 'nightclub'. They were so excited, and got all dressed up. Dad walked them for miles through the dark to a pub right out in the country, and when they got there it was a real spit-and-sawdust place. The highlight of the evening was a local man singing the Americans all 14 verses of D'ye Ken John Peel. They saw the funny side though. Apparently." She thought for a moment. "Then there were the Free French. They were a lot more serious though."

"They had a lot to be serious about."

Her head was full of stories and her eyes shone with the memories.

"You should write this down," I said. "Now. You should go home now and do it."

"I have already about the 1930s. Those were hard times. But nobody would be interested in publishing it."

"If it's about the war years, the Imperial War Museum would be interested."

"That's a good idea," she said. "And I could send them my map. My cousin was in the Chindits in Burma. With the Gurkhas. They taught him to throw the Gurkha knife to take a man's head off. They had to, you know. In the jungle. He felt safe when he was with the Gurkhas. And after the war he gave me his map – the secret map of their positions. I'll send it to the Imperial War Museum." Her bus came and she smiled again. "Thank you."

"It was good to meet you."

Hugh picked me up and drove me to his house in York. I spoke to Claire from there. If I was well enough the following day, I would cadge another lift from Hugh and carry on. If not, Claire would pick me up from there.

I woke the following morning, chest tight, coughing. As Hugh and I ate breakfast, the rain started.

No more, I thought. No more until I'm better.

This bike ride was always going to be in two parts. The first part was the easy bit, preparing me for the rigours of the North. So that was the easy bit over.

I phoned Claire again and waited in Hugh's conservatory,

listening to the rain.

I would go home.

For a while.

I had Man-Flu to beat. But then I had the great mystery of Mid-Life to solve and, of course, England to conquer.

Unfinished business.

I would be back.

End of Part One

Part Two

Day Eleven

Target: 31 miles from Holmfirth to Haworth, via Slaithwaite and Hebden Bridge

I had a ten-day break. I guess I needed it.

A week after I arrived home, I was still coughing and wheezing. On the eighth day I was a bit better. On the ninth, I booked a train ticket to Yorkshire for the following day.

I had cycled through eight counties – Dorset, Somerset, Wiltshire, Gloucestershire, Herefordshire, Shropshire, Staffordshire and Derbyshire – and I only had West Yorkshire, North Yorkshire, County Durham and Northumberland to go. Only. In fact, I had the same distance to do all over again; I was half way. Yorkshire (West and North) was huge and would take me three days to cross. Durham a day and a bit. Northumberland four days. There really was a long way to go.

It was hard to leave home again. Ten days was long enough to get into the routines of work, housework, giving kids lifts and all sorts of real life. But I was desperate to finish what I'd started, and I really wanted to do it in dry weather.

While I'd been at home and at work, the seasons had changed from a sodden Spring (and I use the adjective advisedly) to full-blown Summer. If May was the fifth wettest since 1914, the forecast for early June was hot, hot, hot. It felt like now or never.

I had Sunday to Sunday, eight days, to get to Berwick-upon-Tweed. If I started from Hathersage, I wouldn't have time to finish, so I picked Holmfirth over the border in Yorkshire, and within reach of a railway station. I had been driven over the hills north of Hathersage, and that would do me.

I would start in Yorkshire, and I would see if I could find why Yorkshire folk call their county 'God's own country'. I would keep a close look out for anywhere that might fit the description.

Claire drove me to the station at Carlisle. The whole country had wall-to-wall sunshine. Well, all except us. It rained on the way.

It wasn't that there was a little black cloud up there with my name on it. No, it was that the little black cloud had some sort of global positioning system targeting me.

The 'Settle-Carlisle' railway line cuts through green hills and takes to high viaducts as it crosses the Pennines. The rugged beauty of the views shouldn't have surprised me really, because I'd been on it before, but it did.

I was at one end of a carriage mostly occupied by a tour group. They poked cameras out of windows and listened to their guide telling them how far, how high, and how long it took. Mostly it was too far, too high, too long, and too many men had died to push the line across the Pennines. Many were Irish navvies escaping poverty in Ireland for the mixed blessing of paid work right through the harsh, cold winters on England's backbone.

Leeds station didn't look like God's Own Country when we arrived, late. Also, I missed my train to Huddersfield, which meant that I then missed my connection to Brockholes, my jumping off point for Holmfirth.

This was not good. It was 1.40pm already, and I wasn't going to get to Haworth at all if I also had to cycle south all the way from Huddersfield to Holmfirth.

I took an executive decision. I wouldn't go to Holmfirth. I would cut south-westwards until I hit my route, the NCN Route 68: the Pennine Cycleway.

So I headed out of the station at Huddersfield and was immediately totally lost. Actually, I was not 'lost'. I had rarely been 'lost' in the sense that I didn't know where I was. No, like so many times before, I just didn't know which direction to go. I'm not sure there's a word for that in the English language, probably because we (and I use that in the male voice) rarely do not know which direction to go. But there should be a word. Something like 'discombobulated', which I suspect means something different altogether. And yet it's a good-sounding word, and the feel of it in my head was just what I was feeling. I was, I thought, discombobulated.

"You're lost again then," Scott said.

A taxi-driver's directions and some Zen navigation, and I was climbing up into the Pennines along a gently rising but seemingly endless road towards Meltham. Part way up, I did a bit more Zen navigation and cut across to the Blackmoorfoot Reservoir. What a name. There I found what I was looking for. A blue Route 68 Pennine Cycleway sign. I had a guide.

I'd climbed quite high by now, and Huddersfield lay in a bowl off to the east. The map, though, showed double arrows pointing downhill and suddenly I was dropping steeply and losing all that hard-won height. I landed in Slaithwaite and it occurred to me that I could have just cycled straight here up the valley from Huddersfield.

Slaithwaite seems undecided whether it is a town on the rise or the fall. Old mill buildings press around the valley floor, some full, some empty.

Where Richard Arkwright had shown the way with his water-powered mill, others had followed. All up through these dales of Yorkshire and Lancashire, water-power became the driving force of the industrial revolution. The valleys here with their steep sides and fast-flowing rivers were ideal. These northern towns and cities became the textile capitals of the world, weaving wool from England and cotton either from Britain's growing empire or from the bit that got away in 1776 – the independent United States of America.

It's odd to think that our perceptions of the times are based on Jane Austen's novels – dainty young ladies going to balls, waiting for their suitors to call, staring at bare-torsoed young gentlemen appearing wet from swimming in lakes. That sort of thing. For most of the population, life was nothing like that. Workers in the mills around me here might have had 14-16 hour shifts in dark and dirty buildings. Small children would have been employed to run between machines to tie up broken threads. Elsewhere, other children would have been working down mines, or climbing soot-filled chimneys to clean them from the inside. All for a pittance that would have barely fed them. This was a time of astonishing poverty and hardship for most of the population.

In Slaithwaite's valley floor a canal appeared off to the left, and there were people milling around a green-and-gold painted canal boat. More than milling, I realised. They were drinking tea and eating flapjacks and spilling ice cream down themselves. This wasn't just any canal boat, it was a canal boat café.

"Stop," I said to Scott, and he did, and I ordered tea and a flapjack and an ice cream, and I ate them in reverse order.

The canal was another part of the industrial revolution, supplying the raw materials to the mills and taking away the finished products. This one, the Huddersfield Narrow Canal ('Narrow' because it is half as wide as most), crossed the Pennines to connect Yorkshire and Lancashire. It was the highest canal in the country and also had the longest tunnel: over 3 miles of blackness. There were no motors on the original barges of course, and no tow-paths through the canals, so men would lie on their backs, feet on the roof of the tunnel, and 'walk' the barges through. For three miles.

The Narrow had a fairly short active life. Just as water-power in the mills came to be replaced by steam-power, the canals were made obsolete by the steam trains and railways of the 1840s. A century later Slaithwaite's canal was filled in.

Now though, we have a new national industry. The Council has re-dug the canal because of the tourist potential of connecting the valley to the national network. A pleasant by-product of the Council's decision was me sitting with my feet up drinking tea, eating a flapjack and spilling ice cream down my bike shirt. In reverse order.

Setting off, I was immediately cycling up a steep hill, under a narrow railway bridge, which does tend to make you wobble. Not the best place for a small red car to overtake so that the wing-mirror brushed my arm.

"What the-"

Her number also had a B in it, or something I shouted did, anyway. I added her to The List.

'Steep' doesn't do justice to the hill out of Slaithwaite. This was not only the steepest hill so far, it was also a long one. In principle, I don't get off and walk up hills. I cycle, even if only slowly and with stops to look at views, blow a nose, breathe, or sweat. Any excuse, to be honest. But I was reduced to walking up a good part of this one.

"What are you doing?" Scott asked.

Breathe. Breathe.

"Saving-"

Breathe.

"- my-"

Breathe.

"- breath."

It was at the top of this climb when I recalled that I was now on the second part of my journey. The hard bit. The original idea was that I would build my fitness over the easy bit, so that by the time I reached the Pennines, I would be fighting fit. I would be racing up these hills.

The south is, as we all know, flat, while the north is steep and hilly and full of men in flat caps. It had just been my bad luck that the flat bit hadn't turned out to be quite as flat as it should have been, that I'd had raging Man-Flu, and that the Weather Forecast had been written with Noah in mind.

So if I was now on the hard bit, then this afternoon's 30-something miles up and down stonking-great hills, plus the following days, could conceivably be something of a challenge.

I paused for breath (oh, wonderful euphemism) at the top,

and took in the views.

On the domed ridges above Huddersfield, most of the old stone houses had been renovated and the barns converted. New houses had been built in the same style, with long views across the valleys, while the surrounding fields had beautiful brown horses, well cared for. The few farms that were still farms tended to stand out – cracks in the walls, farm dogs staring out of dirty windows, blackened walls from the industrial smoke – blackened gold really.

With a little strength back in my legs, I cycled off along the ridge heading for the crossing point of the M62.

Sustrans, the designers and builders of the NCN cycle routes, hate A-roads. So do I really. Nasty, unpleasant places to be when you're on a bike. However, Sustrans do tend to make some interesting route decisions as a result. The means of crossing the M62 was one of them.

Now, Sustrans is an excellent organisation. They have a hugely ambitious plan to create 10,000 miles of traffic-free bike routes or way-marked quiet lanes.

The initial plan was a little smaller: 5 miles, which puts the 10,000 into perspective. In 1977 a group of enthusiasts set about converting a 5-mile long old railway line between Bristol and Bath into a cycleway. The group became organised as Sustrans (standing for Sustainable Transport), and in the 1980s they used youth employment programmes to expand all round the country. Old railway lines and canal towpaths provided perfect bike routes, and where these were not available, country lanes were way-marked instead. In 1995 Lottery funding was given to create 6,500 miles of cycleways, and that has now been expanded to 10,000. Without doubt, it will grow again. It is a fantastic scheme. Thank you Sustrans. But the NCN route 68 crossing of the M62, well…

First there was the unlikely sight of a blue sign pointing through a gap in the hedge. Then there was the grassy/rubbly path which seemed to just drop away towards Scammonden Water reservoir below. I followed it down and down, asking various dog-walkers if there was a cycle route here.

"Yes."

"No."

"Errm. Well, there's a narrow footpath along the water's edge. It is a bit narrow though."

Scott said, "You're lost again."

"I'm not. I'm discombobulated."

"You've made that up."

"No, I haven't. Well, not much."

Eventually I realised that I should only have come half way down the grassy/rubbly slope rather than right down to the water, and I pushed and pulled Scott up a different grassy/rubbly slope to a path close to the roaring motorway and we bounced along between motorway on one side and water on the other. The path then turned to go through a dark tunnel under the roaring road above, and up another steep slope on the far side.

I looked at my watch. I'd been going for two hours. I looked at the bike computer. I'd only done 12 miles. This was not good.

The route followed the ridge past the quaintly-named Gallows Pole Hill.

Estate agent: "Can I help you, sir?"

Customer: "I have a house to sell on Gallows Pole Hill."

Estate agent: "I think Smith, Pollett and Grainger might suit you better, sir. They're just down the road, left at Executioner Street, and right at Guillotine Road."

Gallows humour. You can't beat it.

The road dropped down into Sowerby Bridge, another mill town on the cusp of redevelopment. It was a relief to arrive here because I had studied the map. I knew, I absolutely knew, that the route to Hebden Bridge was straight along the valley. Mercifully flat for five miles. So when the sadistic

120

route designers at Sustrans then took me uphill, and more uphill, with no end in sight, I said, "Balderdash" again, and turned round in the road. It was 4 o'clock in the afternoon and I was only half way to Haworth, so I'd take an A-road for the sake of flatness and speed.

A sign appeared, pointing down towards the valley floor: 'Calder Valley Cycleway'. Valley? Valley! Yes. I nosed the bike downhill and was only discombobulated for a short time in a housing estate before the old Zen stuff took me across a playing field, under a tunnel and over a bridge to a canal towpath. Which was flat.

I skidded to a halt by a wooden sculpture that I think had something to do with the Brontë sisters. However, I was so taken up with failing to take a photograph of myself using the timer, that the dedication eludes me. Actually, I didn't fail to take a photograph. It's just that the photograph is mostly of my bum running back towards the sculpture.

The cycle-path led through woods. Flat. Then little lanes and the back of mill-buildings. All flat. So just why does Route 68 go uphill and down dale to get to the same place? On closer inspection, the NCN map does show the Calder Valley Cycleway as an alternative, but well, that's not the same.

Hebden Bridge was once like Slaithwaite and Sowerby Bridge. Mill buildings, back-to-back terraces, in fact, over-the-top terraced houses that climb up the steep valley sides. But Hebden Bridge has been transformed. China shops, antique shops, tea shops, galleries, a cobbled square, people sitting at tables outside the pub drinking wine.

It was 5 o'clock and I would dearly have liked to join them. I didn't think I'd found God's Own Country quite yet, but I'd have loved to go into a hotel, book in, and jot down in the visitors' book: 'expensive but spotless'.

No, I had to go on. I was booked in to Haworth YHA.

I think it was at this point that I noticed something odd. I had cycled for several hours and not got wet.

By way of celebration, I turned the bike towards Haworth. It was eleven miles to Haworth, and I believe that four or five of them were uphill. Continuously uphill. Steeply uphill. No namby-pamby stuff, this was a serious challenge for tired legs. Legs which started to cramp slightly as I got higher.

Oak woods gave way to empty moorland with wide views back over Calderdale, and no sign of the smoke and noise that must have been the common sight of a previous century.

Up again, and again, and again, and finally the top, then steeply downhill the far side, holding on to the brakes as the road zigged and zagged.

In Oxenhope the road levelled and finally contoured around the side of a hill to Haworth, which was wonderful, and I pondered inconclusively why roads don't generally contour around hills. It would make so much more sense.

I was about to cycle down a steep hill into Haworth's town centre to look for the youth hostel, when I saw a grey-haired, grey-bearded man with a rucksack turn off into a housing estate. I know a 'youth' when I see one heading for a hostel. True enough, there was a YHA sign only visible to those coming up the hill.

I should have realised, of course – the YHA would always put their hostel at the top of a hill rather than the bottom if they have a choice.

Howarth YHA looks how a Victorian mill-owner's house in Yorkshire ought to look. Square, grand and sensible all in one. Stained-glass windows above the landing, lots of wood-panelling, and a tradesman's entrance around the back. The sort of house that would call a spade a spade, by 'eck as like.

It was early evening by now, and Scott was happy to rest his weary wheels in the bike shed, while I found my way up a wide flight of stairs to the dormitory.

I sorted out my clothes by my bunk and realised that I had forgotten to pack my non-cycling trousers – the one pair that I was allowed to go out in by my family.

My daughter Suzie had offered to take me shopping for trousers, but it had never quite happened. She and I have a different world-view of shopping. I tend to go shopping when it can no longer be avoided. I don't quite understand shopping as a lifestyle or pastime, unless it involves book shops or outdoor shops or preferably both, rounded off with a cappuccino in a café while reading my new book and pondering my marvellous new boots/waterproof/hi-tech-shirt. I once thought I should read 'Women are from Venus, Men are from Mars', but there was always something else to read that seemed to offer greater philosophical insights. Like 'Round Ireland with a Fridge', for example, or 'The Anglo-Saxon Chronicle'.

The shopping for new trousers hadn't happened because I still had one pair of trousers that didn't have holes and had not suffered from 'shrinking-syndrome'. I may actually get a Nobel Prize for Science for my work on trouser-shrinking-syndrome. I have established as a scientific fact, that when trousers are left unattended in a wardrobe for a long period, the waists shrink. Mine certainly have, and I have conducted an in-depth survey that supports my hypothesis.

I knew what Scott would say, and it involved the phrase 'mid-life crisis'. I decided not to tell him.

Anyway, I didn't have with me the one pair of trousers I possessed without a hole in them or that hadn't shrunk. So my evening attire would have to be the shorts I had ridden in that day, or bike-leggings which look OK on a moving cyclist (I think) but not so good in ordinary life. Lycra is only so flattering on certain shapes and sizes, after all. I decided to order a meal in the restaurant from the cheery YHA girl, rather than walk down the hill into the town to a pub. I wasn't sure that Haworth's pubs were quite ready for me in Lycra.

The only other occupants of the hostel seemed to be an American on a European tour with his two late-teen daughters, and two other men of about my age. That sort of mid-life age. That sort of crisis age.

I was sharing a dormitory with the two men. One was the man I had followed in, who turned out to be a monosyllabic Pennine Way Walker.

Me: "Are you eating here tonight?"

Monosyllabic Pennine Way Walker: "No."

I think he had been on his own too long.

The other was a train-spotter with a head-cold. He had travelled up (by train of course) from Newport in South Wales to look at the Keighley and Worth Valley Railway. Apparently it was used to film 'The Railway Children' and he had always wanted to see it. Not an ambition I shared.

I tried for a while to imagine what combination of attributes I would least like to share a room with, and I must admit that I did struggle to find something other than a Train-spotter with a Head-Cold.

Captain's log: Day Eleven
The day's distance: 32.27 miles / 51.63 Km
The journey so far: 356.18 miles / 569.89 Km
Average speed: 8.5 mph / 13.6 Kmph (easily the slowest
so far, up all those hills)
Maximum speed: 31.0 mph / 49.6 Kmph
Minimum speed: 2.8 mph / 4.48 Kmph

Lying in bed, I decided that I was being unfair to my Train-spotter with a Head-Cold. In fact, he was a nice enough guy, and when he announced to me and to Monosyllabic Pennine Way Walker that he sincerely hoped he wouldn't snore that night, I could really only agree.

Day Twelve

Target: 37 miles from Haworth to Ripon, via Bingley and Fountains Abbey

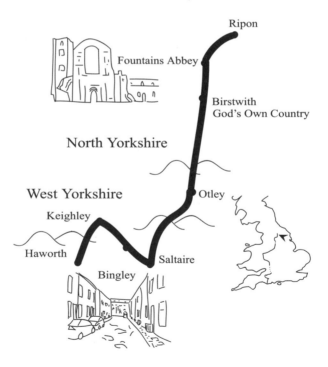

Ripon

Fountains Abbey

Birstwith
God's Own Country

North Yorkshire

West Yorkshire

Keighley

Otley

Haworth

Saltaire

Bingley

Brontë Country was closed.

I was, theoretically at least, a tourist ready to part with good money for a commemorative plate, a Yorkshire tea towel or maybe a CD of Kate Bush screeching something about Wuthering Heights. But just before 9 o'clock on a Monday morning, the shops were closed.

I was in the cobbled main street of Haworth, the sun was shining, and there was only one other person mooching around. Actually, I was fairly certain that this was the best time to be here. I had no doubt that before too long the coaches would arrive, the olde tea shoppes would open, and there would be a roaring trade in Brontë Sisters tea towels. At that moment it was a quiet little cobbled Yorkshire street, well-looked after, and pretty. I liked it, but I strongly suspected that when the shops opened and the coaches arrived, I'd hate it.

The Parsonage, where the Brontë sisters lived and wrote, was also closed, and I was glad about that as well. I didn't want to have to pretend I'd read anything by them. The closest I'd come would have been Kate Bush's 3-minute version, and I suspected that didn't count.

I was looking forward to today, but not because of Tourist Board Brontë Country. I was going to be visiting old haunts. Bingley.

"There are only so many ways you can say that it's going to be hot and sunny." That's what the BBC weather man had said the previous evening. As I retrieved Scott from his lamppost, the sun disappeared. I was already wearing two t-shirts. I added my waterproof.

To get to Haworth's cultural centre, I'd cycled down into the Worth Valley and up the other side. The only thing was, I wasn't altogether sure now which way to go to escape the tea towels. My map wasn't clear, mainly because I didn't know exactly where I was, but it did look as though the lane signposted Oakworth might take me in the right direction.

I was wrong.

Oakworth was down a hugely steep hill, and then up a hugely steep hill. I walked and pushed again, which was a bit depressing for so early in the day.

Looking at the map, I could see exactly where I'd gone wrong. But that wasn't a lot of help.

The BBC man was wrong as well. It was grey and chilly. That black cloud now had my mobile phone number.

I cycled down the main road into Keighley and found it buzzing. Buses were depositing shoppers for Monday morning shopping and workers for Monday morning working.

I was cycling in from the west, and planned on cycling out to the east and then heading south. The signpost for Bingley, however, pointed north. If I hadn't just had the little Oakworth incident, I'd have trusted my Zen navigation. But I didn't. There was a sign, after all.

The sign led me out to the ring road on the north side of town, a busy road which then circled back to the east side of town and almost back to where I had started. If I'd trusted myself, I could have cut through to the same point without touching a ring-road patently unsuited to a banana on a bike. And I mean that in the yellow sense of the word.

The Council then surpassed itself, and a full-sized bike lane appeared on the old main road towards Bingley. I remembered this road during my time here as busy, but now it was quiet-ish, flat and straight.

A sign for the National Trust's East Riddlesden Hall appeared on my right. I had lived just down the road for a year and never visited it. I swung the bike across the road and down the drive past the 'Closed' sign, stopping at the duck pond. Ducks were everywhere, and across the other side was a squat timber-framed building set amongst green lawns, while just outside the walls was Keighley, as un-National Trust a town as I could imagine.

A man on a mower was savaging the lawns, and a lady

arrived in her car looking as though she might work there. Perhaps the Hall wouldn't stay 'Closed', but I thought I'd better press on. I wanted to see what twenty-four years had done to Bingley.

At the age of 23 I'd had enough of work. For some reason known only to Bradford Business School, that suited them as well. They even paid me a grant to go and study there for a year. This was good news. I could escape from a dull job in Birmingham and get myself a useful qualification. Even better, I could be a student again. And that's probably what I wanted most.

So I'd arrived at the Housing Office to find an almighty queue of other late arrivers with no accommodation for the coming year. My heart had sunk as I saw the queue. I could be there for hours.

At the very front of the queue, a skinny, bearded student stepped away from the counter and turned to face the assembled multitudes.

"Anyone want to share a house?" he said.

There was silence, except for shuffling feet.

What the heck, I thought. "Alright," I said. And that's how I moved to Bingley.

The house was a back-to-back terrace house. We could hear the neighbours either side of us, plus the neighbours in the house adjoining our back wall, and in the two diagonally adjoining houses. Mostly we heard a set of neighbours at the back arguing and screaming in the middle of the night. One night she threw him out. Screams. Doors banging. Shouting. Silence. It was a touch unnerving.

The front door had stepped straight out on to broken paving stones and a road of compacted rubble. The outside walls were of a smoke-blackened grit-stone. I think it was called Love Street, but I'm not sure now. It never had a street sign; we always told our friends to turn right at the abandoned white van. I think it was Hugh that came to visit and couldn't find us. The white van had been towed away.

This bit of Bingley, as you can tell, was not posh.

It was warm as I cycled into the back streets of Bingley looking for Love Street. I couldn't find it. It would have helped if the white van had been there.

There were certainly still back-to-back terraces with roads made of rubble. But I think Bingley has been changing. There were new windows in some houses. New doors. Some had had the blackened walls cleaned. One even had a BMW parked outside.

Perhaps the name wasn't Love Street. Or perhaps the whole road had gone. There's a new dual-carriageway by-passing the town centre now, a stone's throw from where I stood. I wondered if Love Street was under tarmac. No Blue Plaque for me here then.

Instead I cycled around to the Leeds and Liverpool Canal, which even in the 1980s had been a draw for tourists.

The 3-Rise Locks had white-painted wood beams on the lock-gates and cobbled paths with neatly cut grass.

Only one thing marred the picture. There was no canal-boat café. No tea, flapjack and ice cream. In any order.

The canal boats were cheerily painted and named of course.

Sueandjoe.

Gone Boatin'.

Happytohaveareallylongslowholidaywithoutvery-
muchtodobutlookattheworldgoby.

"Hi," I said. "Are you going far?"

The lady was of mature years, and to my surprise had an antipodean accent. "Well, just travelling really. We're retired. We're taking four years to travel all round the canals of England."

"Wow."

"We don't travel in the winter. Too cold."

"And you're Australian?"

"Yup. Though my husband's English. We love it. It's so beautiful."

"I wonder, would you mind taking a photo of me on my camera?"

"Sure." She put down her lock-key, abandoning a husband in mid-lock who I think was expecting her to be doing something with the lock-key.

It's funny, I still looked constipated on that photo.

I wasn't.

The backdrop to the photo was the Damart factory, another of the big Yorkshire textile mills. Very unusually, it seemed to still be a factory.

At its peak, the textiles industry of Britain employed hundreds of thousands of people. More than coal. More than steel. More than the car industry.

Leeds, Bradford, Manchester, Halifax, Nottingham, Leicester and many more, were all towns that grew and thrived on textiles. Yet when textiles died as a major British industry, it all disappeared with a whimper and not a bang. There was no equivalent of the miners' strike. And no national beating of breasts such as when steel plants closed, or Rover finally coughed its last breath. There was certainly no equivalent to the Luddites – the followers of a Ned Ludd right here in the West Riding of Yorkshire in the 18th century, who destroyed the new spinning and weaving machines that were taking their jobs.

The few textiles manufacturers that are left in Britain (I must register an interest, working for one of them myself) find it ever harder to compete with imports. Every few weeks another name closes or moves production overseas. It's not just textiles, of course. British manufacturing as a whole has had its own Mid-Life Crisis; a need, I suppose, to accept change, and a reluctance to do so. Now that was a deep thought.

I cycled down the tow-path away from the locks. On the far side were mill buildings unlike any I had seen so far. One had obviously been renovated and was now advertising itself as 'waterside apartments'. Next to it, a brand new building was taking shape. Not just any shape either, but the shape of a Yorkshire mill building, designed from scratch to offer modern luxury apartments.

I said to Scott, "It wasn't like this in my day."

"Is this going to be one of your 'we lived in a paper bag' rants?"

I gave him a look. "Bikes like you don't know you're born," I said. And if we're honest with ourselves, there wasn't much my two-wheeled friend could say to that.

I had been going to take to the hills from Bingley, but Saltaire was so close, and I hadn't been there for twenty-four years. I had to go to Saltaire. It was south-east – the wrong way – but I just had to.

It was a lovely ride. Flat of course, with canal and woods as company for a couple of miles, until a stone-flagged ramp took me up into Titus Salt's town on the river Aire: Saltaire.

Titus Salt was a self-made man. And when he'd made himself, he made Saltaire for his workers.

The middle of the 19th century was a time when consciences were starting to be pricked by the truly awful working conditions in factories and mines. A commission had reported the story of an 8-year-old-girl working in the mines: '*I go out at four and sometimes half past three in the morning, and come home at half past five (in the afternoon). Sometimes I sing when I have a light, but not in the dark; I dare not sing then.*' An 8-year-old. In the mines.

The 1840s ('the hungry forties') for the first time saw women and children prohibited from working in the mines, and their hours cut in factories like those here in Yorkshire – 6 hours for small children, 12 hours for women.

For Titus Salt, none of this was good enough. He built his workers homes. Ordinary workers received houses with a cellar, a pantry, a living room, a scullery and three bedrooms. Overlookers had up to six bedrooms depending on the size of their family.

He built his workers a chapel to pray in, a school to teach their children, a park for them to play in, alms houses to retire into. In fact he provided everything that most mill owners did not. His was a welfare-state before the state provided anything. The only thing he didn't provide, or even allow, was alcohol. There were no pubs or bars. This was an alcohol-free zone.

In the 19th century, Saltaire would have thrived and hummed, but when I had last been here, the town had had a depressing air. The huge mill had been empty, with some of the shops boarded up, and weeds growing between paving slabs.

But if Bingley was changing, Saltaire already had. School groups were following furled umbrellas. Students were disappearing into lectures in a college campus. Tourists were mooching. And there were places to mooch to. The mill now houses a David Hockney Gallery and designer shops, while the row of shops on the main street includes cafés and wine bars. Titus would turn in his grave at the wine bars, especially the name of one: 'Don't tell Titus'.

Along the road a bakers/café offered brunch of scrambled egg and bacon, and that helped me cycle along Caroline Street, past Fanny, Edward, Amelia, and Henry Streets. I turned down Mary Street, and cycled back along Titus Street, passing George Street, Helen Street and the slightly unfortunate Upper Ada Street. I did miss out on Albert, Constance, Shirley and Katherine, but even so it was clear that Sir Titus, as he became, had a lot of children.

I had to leave the canal soon afterwards. The canal was heading further south-east for Leeds; it was time I went north. I could have stayed on valley-floor A-roads, but they were busy and unpleasant. Unfortunately that meant cycling up the hill through Baildon on to Baildon Moor, which was a trifle steep.

I had lunch 2 in the sun at Hawksworth, and did a fresh calculation of my route. Then I did it again. Each time, it suggested that my detour into Saltaire hadn't been the best plan in terms of distance. It now looked like the day would be 45 miles instead of 37, and I'd need to get a shift on to reach Fountains Abbey before it closed.

Still, it was very pleasant sitting there on the bench put up by the good people of Hawksworth, with its steel plaque set in stone to give the distances from my viewpoint. I realised that I was on a ridge attached to Ilkley Moor, and that in fact, with my helmet at my side, I was "baht 'at".

Down through Menston, and up again, only of course to go down all over again, into Otley, where I was temporarily discombobulated.

"Oh, you *are* lost, aren't you?" a young guy said, helpfully, before giving me directions that took me past a riverside park full of school children eating lunch in the sun, and out of town on a B-road heading directly north. Directly north, as in not-contouring-around-the-hills directly north. It soon became apparent what the B stands for in B6451.

A bench appeared towards the top of a hill which on my

map was shown with a black steepness arrow pointing the wrong way.

"Stop," I said to Scott, unnecessarily.

I flopped down on to the bench and the phone rang. I was able to point out to my friend Ian that I had just cycled over a giant black arrow. This ride was hard. Ian, however, was sitting behind a desk and his sympathy was a touch muted.

I'd crossed another border, and was level with Harrogate, crossing moorland. This was North Yorkshire. My ninth county. Three to go. Three big ones.

Instead of West Yorkshire's mills, there were maybe a dozen, giant golf balls. Communications, I thought, and I stopped about a quarter of a mile back to take a photograph. It was a good photograph, with a close-up of the hedgerow – yellow gorse, pink 'red' campion and white hawthorn – and then the golf balls.

It was only when I started cycling past that I realised that the golf balls were inside a serious looking wire fence, with serious looking security cameras, and manned by serious looking guards at the gate. All looking very seriously military.

"Don't look at them," I said to Scott.

"You took a photograph."

"I'll eat it if I have to."

Nothing was shown on my map, so I guess the golf balls don't exist really, and anyone who reads about their existence can expect a dawn raid. Deny everything.

My route stayed high on the ridge, with wispy white cloud against the blue sky, twittery birds, and green, green fields. It was fabulous.

The road then dropped sharply down to the miraculous Dale Post Office and Stores at Birstwith.

It was miraculous partly because it was such a busy little store in a tiny village, but also because it had a bench outside designed for weary cyclists eating ice cream in the sunshine.

Mums and grandmas collected children from the next-door primary school. Farmers picked up groceries. Older residents stopped to chat with younger ones.

This was village life as it used to be. I had found God's own country. It was right here, sitting outside the Dale Post Office and Stores at Birstwith in the sunshine. With an ice cream.

Time was moving on though, so I set off for Fountains Abbey. The hills were less steep, which my legs were glad of. I had Luddite legs by now.

I almost rode right past the back entrance to Fountains Abbey. I was glad I hadn't, because the lady at the gate said I could walk my bike through the grounds and out the Ripon-side gate.

From the 19th century in West Yorkshire, I stepped back in time. First there was a magnificent house. Stone and glass in the shape of an Elizabethan hall. Four or five stories tall, and wider than it was high. Built for pleasure rather than defence. And built partly from what came into view as I moved further back in time – the austere skeleton of Fountains Abbey itself.

I wheeled Scott across the grass towards ruins. Tall pillars carried high arches that no longer had a roof. The floor was gone, grass now, and wild flowers were growing from cracks in the sandstone.

There was not the same romance as at Wenlock Priory, but it was certainly dramatic.

The monastery was founded here by thirteen monks who had failed in their attempt to reform their own monastery in York, and been expelled. They were given this land 'more fit for wild beasts than men to inhabit', and lived lives devoted to prayer and silence.

The monks themselves lived frugal lives, but the monastery also employed lay workers, and these made good use of the gifts and donations given to the abbey. Fountains became one of the richest of England's abbeys, owning huge estates stretching from the Lake District up to Teeside.

When Henry VIII's men closed Fountains, it fell into ruin in the same way as Wenlock Priory. By the 18th century it had been acquired by the neighbouring estate of Studley Royal. The new English passion for landscaping led to the creation of gracious gardens for gracious living, and the ruins became the backdrop.

Sort of a big rockery.

I wheeled Scott past the rockery, and there was the pond. Well, a bit bigger than a pond. Water gardens, complete with follies and temples and statues.

We came here when Claire was pregnant with Lisa. Claire was actually very pregnant, and her trousers were very white. We had wandered down a path next to one of the lakes. This lake, however, had been drained and was dried mud. (You might be starting to see a connection with the white trousers now.)

A swan's nest was blocking our path, with a defiant-looking swan guarding it. There was no way around the nest without walking on the dried mud. Gallantly, I placed a foot on the mud. It was quite solid, and I led the way around.

"It's fine," I said.

Claire followed, shoes placed where mine had been.

There was a shriek behind me, and I turned to find her sunk up to her thigh. The dried mud had in fact been a dried crust on top of otherwise very wet and sticky mud.

She was not altogether pleased.

I helped her out, but at one stage she did put her foot back down into the mud to retrieve her shoe.

She was not altogether pleased all over again.

Claire now had one mostly-dry white leg with a mostly clean shoe, and one horribly claggy brown leg with a sodden mess on the end of it. I seem to recall it was quite a long walk back to the car, where we didn't have a change of clothes.

Personally, I blame the swan.

Scott said, "So was it in the newspapers? 'Young father-to-be strangled with muddy trousers'."

"Thank you for that thought."

The Ripon exit from Fountains Abbey was a long straight lane through woodland that framed a view down to Ripon cathedral. A herd of deer meandered across the road in front of me, and I crept close to try for a photo. Too close. They skittered away.

The bike computer was saying 400 miles for the whole trip to date and nearly 45 for the day, so I let my Luddite legs cruise gently for the couple of flat-ish miles into Ripon.

I had forgotten my directions to the B&B, so I phoned and spoke to 'Geoff' who sounded like a delightful elderly chap, and that is exactly what he turned out to be.

"I'm afraid things are starting to fall apart a bit," he said. "Bit like me."

He was right. A net curtain fell off when its Sellotape broke.

None of the fitments could really be described as new, or even nearly new. But then Geoff wasn't new either. The house was a reflection of him. And nothing the matter with that.

Scott was in the garage for the evening, and I pottered down the road into the market square.

This was, I decided, the best city I had been in so far.

There had only been two, of course, but Ripon was doing fine if it nudged Wells off the top spot.

In fact, it was wonderful that evening, with the sun shining into a broad market place, from which the cars had been shunted off to the edges. The buildings around were varied and venerable, stone, brick and timber-frame cheek-by-jowl. The Wakeman's House was 16th century, the Town Hall 18th century, and where the 20th or 21st centuries had intruded, they had done so with a nod to the past and the character of Ripon.

There was even a 1911 cabman's shelter – like a little wooden tram, raised on legs – and now used as a gathering point for guided walks.

I strolled through lanes to the cathedral, and here the beautiful west front was glowing from the setting rays of the sun. There were no towers, or spires, or panoramas of angels and kings, but it was a perfectly proportioned golden stone frontage. A welcome that I would see again properly the following day. Tonight, though, I needed food.

A Chinese restaurant looked out on the square and offered me a window seat. I watched the comings and goings, and sat too long to hear the Wakeman's (or watchman's) horn which is apparently still blown at 8 o'clock each night to mark the start of the curfew. But across the front of the Town Hall, above the tall arched windows of the ground floor and the pillared first floor, I was able to read in large gold letters:

EXCEPT YE LORD KEEPETH YE CITTIE,
YE WAKEMAN WAKETH IN VAIN

You can't argue with that, I thought.

I wandered back to Geoff's, where I refrained from using the exercise bike in my room. True, my legs were rather tired after my exertions on a real bike, but I also suspected it might be held together by Sellotape.

I went to bed thinking partly about how much I liked Ripon, partly about twenty years ago at Fountains Abbey,

Captain's log: Day Twelve
The day's distance: 47.89 miles / 76.62 Km
The journey so far: 404.07 miles / 646.51 Km
Average speed: 9.9 mph / 15.84 Kmph
Maximum speed: 33.5 mph / 53.6 Kmph

and those white trousers.

Day Thirteen

Target: 41 miles from Ripon to Brompton-on-Swale, via Middleham and Richmond

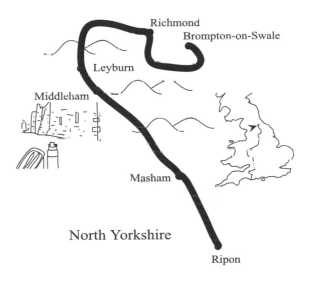

I apologised to Geoff for the Sellotape / net curtain incident. He didn't look altogether surprised, and I imagined this same scene happening every day. Geoff probably went straight upstairs and re-balanced the net curtain and the tape in time for his next guest.

Scott had been fine in the garage, and we cycled back into town. This was 'the cathedral city of the Dales', and I really wanted to see the cathedral.

The market square was just as pleasant in the morning as the evening – busy and sunny. It didn't actually feel part of the Dales though; there were more brick buildings than stone ones. This felt like lowland Yorkshire – a sister city of York itself perhaps.

The cathedral doesn't cater for bicycling pilgrims – I struggled to find where to chain Scott to. The building was maybe not the most spectacular of my journey, but then I had high standards after the west front of Wells and those scissor arches, and also the high, painted roof at Sherborne Abbey. But it was homely, somehow, and there were some things I was very taken with.

There were a dozen or so painted statues inside the church – the reds, golds and purples that at Wells would have covered the whole west front but were now bare stone. There were also little wooden carvings on the seats of the choir. One is of a rabbit running down a hole, and is said to be the inspiration for Alice in Wonderland.

My favourite part of the cathedral, however, was the plainest part of it. The crypt was part of the original church on this site, dated at 672AD, so very early Anglo-Saxon. In the 7th century, Ripon was in the independent Kingdom of Northumbria. Its people were mostly pagans. We still have echoes of those days. Wednesday is really Woden's Day. Thursday is Thunor's Day. Friday is Freia's Day. Thunor – or Thor as the Vikings called him – is (and was then) everyone's favourite of course, beating his hammer to make thunder, riding his chariot across the sky to move the sun, bringing luck to those who sacrificed to him. You definitely wanted Thunor on your side.

But by the second half of the 7th century, Anglo-Saxon Kings were being converted by either Scottish monks from Iona and Lindisfarne, or by monks following the Roman version of Christianity. Once a King was converted, the task of these monks became so much easier. They were invited to build churches and to form monasteries, and one of them was exactly where I was standing – the crypt of the church created by an Anglo-Saxon by the name of Wilfrid.

Stone steps led me down to a small whitewashed room with an arched roof, arched doorways and little shelves set into the wall for candles. Not a crypt for family burials this; the Anglo-Saxon crypt was used to house holy relics. A place of mystery for quiet worship.

What a force Wilfrid was. In 664, the King had called together representatives of the Scottish church and also representatives of the more formal and strict persuasion – the Roman church. In a great debate at Whitby, the Roman cause was argued by Wilfrid, and he won the day.

Wilfrid went on to fall out with and antagonise a whole string of other Christians in his quest to bring Roman Christianity to the English Kingdoms. But he kept on going, and as Bishop of York, one of his achievements was the creation of new monasteries and churches to convert the pagans and the non-Roman Christians. Wilfrid – St Wilfrid – is one of the reasons that Anglo-Saxon England became Christian.

I have no doubt that Wilfrid would have stood where I was, on the exact same spot. Head tonsured to baldness at the back. Ignoring the itchy undyed wool of his long robe. Berating any who did not absolutely agree with him.

I suspect St Wilfrid was a bit scary.

Back in the market square, I bought sandwiches and

biscuits for lunch, found a bench in the sun, and ate all the biscuits. That's what I do.

As I sat there, I decided that I'd had enough of big hills. For today anyway. I studied the map. Instead of the way-marked lanes through the foothills of the Pennines, I could take an A-road through Masham, Middleham and Leyburn all the way to Richmond. And to be fair, an A-road linking Ripon and Richmond wasn't going to be over-busy.

I wasn't altogether certain which way the A-road was, of course.

I retrieved Scott and looked around for any useful signs. I didn't find any. I'd ask.

A teenage girl didn't appear to have even heard of Masham.

A lady of slightly more mature years looked at me in a Yorkshire sort of way, and said, "It's not Mash-ham. It's Mass-'em."

"Ah, that explains…"

She pointed beyond the market square. "Left at t'clock in t'middle o't'road."

I thought I probably understood her, but even if I didn't, I decided not to discuss t'directions any further. I'd take t'left t'urn and hope for t'bes't'.

"Say nowt," I told Scott in my best Yorkshire. Which, to be honest, isn't particularly good.

My road into Ripon had been leafy and pleasant, and my road out was the same.

The countryside rippled, as though the Pennines away to the left had been thrown down into Yorkshire's soil, and the wavelets had reached here and just fossilised in the sunshine. The colours of the day were vigorous and bright. This was grain country, and the growing green wheat was laced with orange-red poppies and yellow buttercups (at least I think that's what the yellow things were), while the hedgerows were filled with red campion and something purply-blue and tall.

144

I would just point out that I gave up Biology at age 13.

Above was a proper sky-blue, with puffy white clouds holding back some of the heat of the day. I was cycling through a painting.

I sailed through pretty North Stainley and was about to do the same with an equally pretty West Tanfield when I noticed an English Heritage sign for a 15th century tower. A quick tour of a dark ruin and I was away again. This was fabulous cycling, easy compared to what had gone before and to what I would have to go back to. An interlude. My spirits were high. I liked North Yorkshire.

There was one downside. North Yorkshire seemed to be top of the roadkill league table. Perhaps they have more rabbits than the rest of the country. Or perhaps they don't teach them how to cross roads in rabbit-school here. I decided to take things into my own hands, and shouted at rabbits in the grass verges as I passed them.

"Rabbits!" I shouted at some.

"Get OFF the road," I shouted at others.

It seemed to work. Where they had ignored me on a quiet bike, they now scampered off into the fields. I was a hero to rabbit-kind.

I was less of a hero to a young and exceptionally friendly couple on a footpath close to one little rabbit.

"Go on, get out of it. Oh, er, sorry," I said. "I meant the rabbits."

Before I knew it I was in a place of pilgrimage. Where modern man comes to see how what he values most has been created. And to buy some bottles of it. Yes, this was the home of the brewery tour.

The Theakstons and Black Sheep breweries are both in Masham. The former was briefly owned by a multinational but bought back by a descendent of the 19th century founder Robert Theakston. The latter was founded by other members of the Theakston family in 1992. And the Theakston clan do seem to know how to brew good beers.

"Black Sheep?" Scott asked.

"It's half past ten in the morning."

"So when do you prefer your Black Sheep?"

"Can bikes be neutered?"

I parked up in the market square, another enormous one, with character-filled Yorkshire-stone buildings all round. The reason for the size of the market square goes back to wool again. This was where the great flocks of medieval sheep were brought for sale – as many as 80,000 sheep at one time.

There was something wrong here though. The car ruled, with benches plonked into the middle of what had become a giant car park.

Well, mostly the car ruled. Where it didn't, litter did.

'Masham-shire is too pretty to litter' said the sign, but the bins were full and over-flowing. Litter was scattered around the seats. Chip wrappers and polystyrene cups were everywhere.

Mass-'em could be a lovely little town, but I felt no inclination to linger. I'd been going to have a cup of tea, but instead cycled on. So, you Tourist Authority of Masham-shire, you missed serious tea-spending money that day. The mystery shopper didn't shop.

Not far on, I was distracted by an ice cream farm. Bryfords, with no litter, but cows, a shop, picnic benches, toilets and a family whose 3-year-old was going for the world record in how much ice cream could be smothered on a face. He was doing well.

I went for raspberry and cheesecake flavour and decided on balance to eat it rather than smother it all over my face.

Just down the road, I bypassed Jervaulx Abbey. Sorry, Jervaulx, but I'd just stopped for an ice cream, and Richard III was beckoning from Middleham.

Approaching the town of Middleham, the ripples in the

landscape started to get a bit ripply-er and the sun had started the farmers off with their hay-making.

Middleham was a little stone-built village on the side of a hill, complete with pubs, cobbles and a stepped market-cross from which red, white and blue bunting stretched across to the surrounding houses. The bunting was a nice touch, and I wondered how word of my arrival had reached them.

According to the town sign, Middleham was twinned with Agincourt, the scene of the Battle of Agincourt, one of England's greatest victories (England 1 France 0), alongside the Battle of Wembley in 1966 (England 4 Germany 2) and the Battle of Waterloo in 1815 (England 2 Abba 0).

What the village hid was its history. Behind the small market square stood the ruins of one of the great castles of medieval England. In its day it was magnificent. The artist's impressions on the postcards in the ticket office showed a castle resembling the Tower of London. Tall, stately, and strong. High outer walls surrounding a large central keep, laid out with halls and staterooms for its owners, the Neville family, and specifically in the 15th century, the Earl of Warwick.

Warwick was so powerful that he was known as the 'Kingmaker', even holding the King prisoner right here in Middleham for a few months. This was the period now known as the Wars of the Roses, in which one half of the royal family battled the other for the kingdom. Yorkist (White Rose) versus Lancastrian (Red Rose).

The Earl was also uncle to a young Duke of Gloucester named Richard, who I had last met at his home in Ludlow, where he is known as the hunch-backed arch-villain of this time, the murderer of his nephews in the Tower of London. Richard was partly brought up in Middleham castle by his uncle, and married his benefactor's daughter. When Warwick died without a son, Richard was given the castle and estates by the King.

A wooden ramp took me up to a viewing platform in the central keep. The walls were thick and strong, but the roof and windows were gone, and the ruins were a sad reflection of the powers that had built them.

Richard became the leading light in the Yorkist camp, bringing up his son in Middleham, developing his own private army, and strengthening the castle as his base in the north.

The wars ebbed and flowed, Yorkist King followed Lancastrian King and then switched back. In 1483 Richard seized the throne and named himself King Richard III, his path cleared by the disappearance of his nephews, the 'Princes in the Tower'.

A year after he took the throne, his son Edward died here, and then a year after that, his wife Ann.

I parked myself in a quiet spot behind the outer walls and got out sandwiches and a drink. The racing stables behind me had horses jumping at each other, chasing one away from the pack. Maybe that was the spot where Richard had kept the horses that Shakespeare had him bemoaning on the battlefield at Bosworth, when his enemies brought him down two years later. 'A horse, a horse, my kingdom for a horse'.

I had seen Shakespeare's Richard III from the front row

of a theatre. The actors came to the stage right past me. Their cloaks brushed my knee, their swords flashed feet from my face, while the brilliant cut-and-thrust of the bard's words was spell-binding. Shakespeare's Richard III was such a bad man, killing and murdering his way to the throne. He got his comeuppance at the end though, as he died on the battlefield, the play echoing a story from the time that his crown was lifted from a thorn bush to be placed on the Lancastrian Henry Tudor's head.

There's a possibility that Middleham Castle does not host that particular play too often.

Once Richard's power was gone from Middleham, the castle decayed and fell into the ruins I was pottering around.

I strolled back towards the entrance to look at the white marble statue of Richard III. The sculptor had given the King high cheek-bones and narrow eyes, a crown on his long hair, a cloak, tights and a cricket-box. There was no hunch-back, but also, strangely, no arms. This was an attribute that the historians must have overlooked. Or I suppose the sculptor might not be able to do hands. Or maybe English Heritage's budget ran out when the sculptor reached the shoulders. Either way, it seemed a little odd, but then Yorkshire folk have always argued that Richard III was just misunderstood.

Scott was waiting patiently just outside the gates. "A horse, a horse," I said.

"Do you want to walk home?"

The road took me down to cross the meandering river Ure coming out of Wensleydale, and then up a long hill into the town of Leyburn. It wasn't a steep hill, but the day was very hot now, and I could feel the sun burning through.

Leyburn was busy. Where Middleham Castle had originally been built to defend the route up into the Pennines via Wensleydale, Leyburn had grown alongside the road to supply the valley. The land rose again the other side of Leyburn and

I felt I was back in the Pennines. The scenery became more rugged and starker, with smaller fields, beef cattle and sheep. Pheasants strolled nonchalantly across the road and in the fields either side, with their goldy-russet plumage in a colour which I think should be named 'Target' and their distinctive cry of 'shoot-me-shoot-me'.

Signs appeared for events in Swaledale, and it occurred to me how many dales I was crossing – Calderdale, Airedale, Wharfedale, Wensleydale, Swaledale – with more to come. Up one side of the valley, over the top, down again the other side, and then repeat the process. I was cycling across the grain of the land. No wonder there were so many blooming hills. Who planned this route, anyway?

My gears stuck a few times as I did some ups and downs, and a couple of times I almost ground to a halt.

"Hey, Scott, what are you doing?"

"Me?"

"You."

"You're the one with the oil."

"Ah," I said.

Swaledale turned out to be a dramatic contrast to the soft grain-land around Ripon. There were woods, low cliffs and a young river with water tumbling over rocks in small water-falls and rapids. The road shadowed the river gently down-hill for several miles, only leaving the riverbank to climb into the town of Richmond.

I was funnelled into the massive market square. Truly massive, but unfortunately another market square which has been devoted to the automobile. I was looking for a pavement café in the sunshine to have an ice cream and a sit down, but there were cars and busses parked higgledy-piggledy across the whole of it. Double-yellow lines and white parking boxes obscured the cobbles, and ugly green wheely-bins surrounded the church-turned-museum in the middle of the square. An ice cream van by a tall stone obelisk only showed what the town was missing; there were families sitting on the uncomfortable stone steps of the obelisk eating their ice creams or drinking from cans. It was such a wasted opportunity. I would see if the castle had a café instead.

It didn't, but it did have a coffee machine. I couldn't work it, of course, but a kind English Heritage lady took pity and I took coffee on to the great grass lawn inside the walls of Richmond Castle.

To be honest, there isn't a great deal to see inside the castle. It sits on a hill above the river, so the views are tremendous down to the water, but of the castle itself, not much remains but the outer wall. There is a new garden being planted, and the oranges and purples of flowers and shrubs against the ruined castle walls made good photographs.

Richmond Castle was built to defend Swaledale, just as Middleham defended Wensleydale, but the most interesting part of the museum was the castle's role in the First World War.

This was a prison used for conscientious objectors refusing to fight for King and Country. The 'Richmond 16' were to be made an example of and were illegally spirited off to France where they were put before a tribunal on trumped up charges, sentenced to death, and then told that their sentences would be reduced to ten years hard labour. The rooms where they were kept in Richmond still have the fairly unusual graffiti of religious icons and poems.

There is also a story that a local man, Potter Thomson, discovered a vast underground hall beneath the castle where he found King Arthur and his knights lying asleep on a stone table. I tapped on a few walls before I left the castle, but none of them sounded hollow.

"Hello?" I called.

"Hello," the English Heritage lady said.

"Ah, yes, just, um…"

I cycled off towards my camping barn at Brompton-on-

Swale via Catterick Garrison. This turned out to be a mistake because they are in entirely different directions. I blamed the map. Scott blamed me.

I should have realised when I crossed the River Swale that I was actually cycling to Brompton-**on-Swale** and that cycling steeply uphill away from the river was probably not the quickest route.

Catterick Garrison is huge. It's really an army town rather than an army camp. I particularly liked the names of the roads – Montgomery, Smuts, French and so on – all named after generals. Just like my grandfather, whose Christian names were Robert French Hector, named of course after Generals Roberts, French and Hector in the Boer War.

Finding no signpost for Brompton-**on-Swale,** I stopped for directions. Brompton-**on-Swale** turned out to be some way further on, then left and then, well, part way back towards Richmond alongside the River **Swale**. I continued to blame the map. Scott didn't.

The route was at least mostly downhill from Catterick Garrison, which is one advantage of having cycled uphill.

I phoned Mrs Wilkins at the YHA camping barn for directions.

"Oh, you're coming this time, are you?"

"Ah, yes, sorry."

I had been booked in previously and had not let them know about my episode of Man-Flu / plague. I was suitably apologetic.

Mr and Mrs Wilkins opened the camping barn in 1992, converting the outbuildings into three dormitories upstairs and a large lounge/kitchen downstairs. It was really quite comfortable, particularly since I was the only one staying that night.

Again.

Had word got around?

I wheeled Scott into the kitchen.

"People still don't know about camping barns," Mrs Wilkins said when she brought me out a pot of tea on a tray.

Which is a pity, because it is infinitely better than real camping. Don't expect luxury, and bring a sleeping bag with you, but they're fine. For the travelling cyclist or walker in the Pennines (and this one is close to the Coast to Coast walking route), they are brilliant. This barn even had duvets, which meant that my daughter's sheet sleeping bag was just right. Thank you, Lisa.

Mr Wilkins was mending a big hay-making attachment for the tractor just outside the barn door.

"Is this a busy time of year?" I asked

"That rain in May smashed all the hay down," he said, "but the heat and sun have brought it up again."

"I know the feeling," I said.

There was a kitchen in the barn, but I had no cookable food with me, and so set off to walk to the village pubs.

"We don't do food on Tuesdays," the first landlady said, "but I can phone the Chinese and get them to deliver."

The second landlady said, "We're only doing soup and sandwiches because we're moving the kitchen."

This was a blow. I was hungry, and the Farmers Arms was apparently ten minutes away.

"There's an hour's wait," the landlord of the Farmers Arms said, ten minutes later.

I had no choice. "I'll have a pint of Black Sheep while I'm waiting."

"The Black Sheep's off."

"Old Speckled Hen?"

"Old Speckled Hen."

"And Thai Chicken in an hour?"

The Thai Chicken was delicious. So was the Old Speckled Hen. Good poultry country, obviously.

Back at the barn at 9.30, there was still a lot going on, with people moving in and out of the sheds. It might be an early morning as well. 'Make hay while the sun shines,' I suspected. I bolted the outside door and headed to bed.

Captain's log: Day Thirteen
The day's distance: 42.22 miles / 67.55 Km
The journey so far: 446.29 miles / 714.06 Km
Average speed: 11.5 mph / 18.4 Kmph
Maximum speed: 30.5 mph / 48.8 Kmph

Darkness. Drowsyness. Sleep.

Banging at the outer door.

Ignore it.

Louder banging.

Light on and struggle to the door.

Two men, one older, one younger.

"Are you staying tonight?" I said. "I thought I was by myself."

"We came while you were out. Been to the pub."

"The ones without food?"

"That's the ones."

Day Fourteen

Target: 44 miles from Richmond to Castleside, via Staindrop and Raby Castle

Northumberland

Castleside

Wolsingham

Hamsterley Forest

Raby Castle

Staindrop

The Pennines

County Durham

Richmond

Brompton-on-Swale

North Yorkshire

I emerged into full sunlight from the dark dormitory to find my night-time visitors already packing up to leave. They were father and son. Actually they were Yorkshiremen, so I need you to imagine the 'a' in father sounding like the 'a' in dad, and the 'o' in son sounding like the 'ou' in could. That's relatively easy if you're from Yorkshire, of course.

Faather was 50-ish and completely bald, with a reddened head and a chunky body. Suun was 20-ish, tall and fit-looking. Neither, though, looked very happy.

My Sherlock Holmes deductions led me to a question. "You walking?"

Faather looked up from putting walking boots on. "Aye. T'coast to coast. But it's blooody haard."

It seemed they'd bought new boots from an outdoor shop, taking the advice of the shop on which to buy. Now they were regretting it.

"We spent a oondred and fifty pounds each on these and there's no give in t'souls at all," faather said.

"They mek your feet feel noom after 'alf an hour walking."

It didn't help that in this red-hot weather they were carrying full camping gear – tent, stove, sleeping bags and food. Their rucksacks were enormous. They both looked exhausted.

"How far are you going today?"

"Nineteen mile," faather said. "I don't think we'll mek it. Boogar this faather-suun-bonding." He turned to his son. "I don't mean it."

"You blooody do," suun said.

They'd gone by the time I'd had a breakfast of cereal bars and an apple, and had packed up my kit. I wheeled Scott outside.

"Well?" Scott said.

"Oil?"

"Tyres while you're at it."

I oiled the chain and gears, blew up the tyres and pretended I knew what I was doing when I examined the brakes.

Scott said, "Don't think you're doing any bonding with me."

"Aye," I said.

I took the direct route back to Richmond, which ambled alongside the River Swale past the ruins of Easby Abbey. There's a legend that in the 18th century a tunnel was discovered in Richmond Castle leading in the direction of the abbey. The tunnel was too small for any of the men to fit down, so a drummer boy was sent. The soldiers followed the sound of his drumming almost as far as the abbey, before the drumming suddenly stopped. I do hope that it's just a legend.

The day was heating up as I climbed a long hill into Richmond with a glorious view across to the castle on its rocky perch above the river. There were no clouds at all, and I could feel the heat of the sun on the backs of my legs and my arms already. It was going to be a full-sun-screen day.

In Richmond I was looking for a B-road heading north. I asked directions and went about half a mile west before Zen clicked in. I took some more directions, turned round, and went north.

The road went through pretty Gilling West with its little village green and its ladies tending their flower-filled gardens. Just beyond the village, half a dozen horses were being led at a trot along the road by bare-chested lads with big smiles. The horses looked in perfect condition, and I knew who these must be even before I came to the traditional gypsy caravans in the lay-by further on. The caravans had blue-green canvass covers, polished wood and brass fittings.

Some adults were sitting in deck-chairs by the caravans drinking tea. I nodded at one and he raised his mug to me. Fellow travellers; though these ones would be on their way to the Appleby Horse Fair and not to Berwick-upon-Tweed.

It astonished me that they would be taking their horses and flimsy caravans across the Pennines on the A66 to Appleby in Cumbria. It was a fast, fast road, a dual carriageway. Not for the faint-hearted, and I hoped that my fellow travellers would be OK.

It was a long hill up to the A66 ahead of me and I stopped under trees for a cool off before completing it. I was drinking copiously.

The A66 marked the start of a plateau with huge fields of rape just coming into bright yellow bloom, and of still-green wheat. This would have been sheep country in centuries gone by, with the sheep driven down drove roads to the sales of Richmond. Only when I reached little Caldwell were there a few sheep left, and here the shearing had started.

The sun-drenched colours on the plateau were sharp – the green and yellow rape in the fields, the white of the hawthorn hedges, and the bright wild flowers at the roadsides in their pinks, yellows and blues. It occurred to me that I must be in County Durham. It seemed an awfully long way from Dorset, yet I still had days to go, and I was back in the hills with a vengeance.

The road dropped steeply down through woods and then suddenly the views opened out either side of a wide bridge. I stopped at the far end and walked back. Upriver the water was broken by small islets with trees and bushes, and the water tumbled over rocks in broken white water. Downriver was a peacock-blue reflection of the sky, studded with silver-grey rocks, and each bank was emerald-green with full-leafed trees. It was stunning.

A small car crossed the bridge slowly and pulled into a lay-by. An elderly couple walked back towards me.

"Beautiful, isn't it?" the man said.

He had a small pair of binoculars in one hand, and he leaned on the parapet to steady himself as he gazed through them along the river bank.

"Gorgeous," I said. "I hadn't expected such a big river here. I can't really think where I am."

"It's not Wensleydale," the lady said. "I can't think which is the next one up."

"Are you having a day out?" I asked her.

"No, we're on our way to Scotland, but the A66 is closed. There's been an accident."

"Oh," I said. And I thought, I hope it's not my fellow travellers with their caravan and horses. Later, after I arrived home, I learned that the accident had indeed been a car hitting a gypsy caravan. I don't know if it was the man who raised his mug to me, or the laughing bare-chested boys with their horses.

"We're going to the Isle of Mull," the man said. "Bird-watching."

"The sea eagles?"

"Hope so."

They headed back to the car, and I opened out my map to see which river could be so captivating. The lady walked back carrying her road atlas just as I found it.

She said, "It's the Tees," and she was right. This graceful stretch of water would end up in Teesside at Middlesbrough as a very different river.

I cycled up the hill to Winston desperate for a cup of tea after 20 hot miles. Winston was too small for a tea shop though, and I cycled on. As the road bent towards Staindrop the bird-watching couple were pulled in. The man was leaning on the car following a bird with his binoculars. His wife was still in the car.

I stopped beside him. "Seen something?"

He paused, intent on his quarry, then put his binoculars down. "Just a crow," he said with a smile.

He got back in the car. His wife was still sitting there. It occurred to me that only one of them might be the bird-watcher. The other might be the bird-watcher's wife, and it might be a long taxing drive up to Mull as a bird-watcher's wife given the progress they were making.

Staindrop was down the hill from Winston, and was big enough for a tea shop. I located it then mosied up one side of a large village green that runs the length of the village, and back down the other side. South Green and North Green. The grass was long and daisy-filled, with rows of ash and horse chestnut trees for shade.

Along the lanes at the sides of the green, the houses were a grey sandstone, mostly rough-cut though the posher ones were constructed of smooth blocks of stone. Either way, it was a pleasant little place, and the tea shop already had two cyclists inside.

I ordered an early lunch and chatted to the cyclists. Serious ones these, in Lycra tops and shorts, out for a spin from Darlington on serious road bikes. I decided to let them go on ahead of me. Wouldn't want to show them up.

My next stop was just two miles away, and I had been looking forward to this one. I had seen Raby Castle from the road many times, and it was clearly a proper lived-in medieval castle. Big walls. Gatehouse. Portcullis. Moat. Like Middleham and Richmond, only still lived in. The Lord and Lady probably had whole hogs roasted on a spit each night in the great hall, while being entertained by jesters in red-and-yellow costumes with bells on their hats.

It wasn't at all cheap to go in the castle. It had better be good and medieval, I thought, and cycled in.

Today was Wednesday, and the castle is only open on Wednesday and Saturday in June, and then only in the afternoon. Half an hour's time, in fact.

The car park was a field by the lane, and I left Scott chained to a fence. I was the only cyclist there, and it occurred to me that at castles and abbeys and cathedrals up and down England, that had been the case. It wasn't the same with tea shops. I'd met cyclists in tea shops in Somerset,

Shropshire and County Durham. Must be something about cyclists and tea shops.

I wandered in to the stable block while I waited for the castle to open. There were beautifully-kept open carriages there, all polished brass and bright paint, and a guide. His eyes sparkled as I asked him about the carriages. These were 18th and 19th century carriages, including the state coach used by Lord and Lady Barnard for the coronation parade.

I thought a moment. "1953 then?"

"No. 1906," he said in a slight north-east accent. I was beyond Yorkshire now.

"Ah. That one."

He was wonderfully enthusiastic, and he told me about leaf-springs giving suspension for the carriages on the bumpy un-tarmac'd roads; about four-day journeys to London on gloriously padded leather seats for their Lordships; and about the footmen sitting outside at the back of the carriage and the postillion riding one of the horses, each of them outside in all weathers on that four day journey. I thought about the rain I'd had in Derbyshire and about the lack of proper waterproofs in the 18th and 19th centuries, and I sympathised.

"So what brought you here?" I asked.

He looked a little taken aback. I'd asked him about himself, and not about leaf-springs and padded leather seats.

"I retired from the RAF and I live in the village. I was asked if I'd like to do a couple of afternoons a week. What a job, though. I'd do it for free."

I wondered if the owners of Raby Castle knew what a gem they have. As I went out I saw his reading material for the quiet times: The Encyclopaedia of Horsemanship.

I took a quick tour of the prettily cultivated gardens with their glimpses through to the medieval stronghold, and then it was time to go in.

Raby Castle was another stronghold of the Neville

family, the greatest of the northern families alongside the Percy family of Northumberland. (Neville and Percy – this sounds like a Harry Potter book.) But Raby Castle was not lost to the Nevilles in the Wars of the Roses like Middleham was. The family rose again, and this was their power-base. They owned and ruled huge swathes of northern England from this castle, and it was maybe that power which persuaded them that they could take on the Queen of England, Elizabeth I.

The Nevilles had never renounced their adherence to Rome, and in 1569 they were the ringleaders of the Rising of the North in favour of the Catholic Mary Queen of Scots against the Protestant Elizabeth. In the great hall of this castle they gathered around themselves the nobility of the north. The rising was crushed, and the Neville family with it. The king-makers, the lords of the north, were destroyed. Raby was forfeited to the crown, and when the castle was sold off the following century, it was not to the Nevilles but

to the Vane family, who have owned it ever since.

I showed my ticket at the gatehouse and walked under the black-painted portcullis, with the castle itself appearing massively behind. An archway led into a central courtyard. All nicely medieval. But then I went inside, and suddenly this was not a medieval castle anymore. I had fallen through a time warp into the 18th or 19th century. The rooms were extraordinarily opulent – with gold leaf wherever gold leaf might go, countless family portraits, huge crystal chandeliers, and elegant furniture. It had been a while since a hog had been spit-roasted in the great hall. Time had emphatically moved on in Raby Castle.

"Goodness," I said to one of the hovering guides in a particularly grand room. She was an older lady, smartly dressed. "There's been some money here over the years. Where does it come from?"

"The family have always married well. Heiresses."

"Ah. And do they still own a big estate?"

"Well, yes. When you're outside, most of the farmhouses you see painted white belong to Lord Barnard. And the village of course."

"Does Lord Barnard have children?"

"Yes. Five, but of course the estate is entailed. He has one son."

"Sorry, what does 'entailed' mean?"

"That it can only pass through the male line."

"Oh, so there are four girls and one boy, but if it had been five girls, none of them would have inherited?"

"That's right. It would have gone to Lord Barnard's cousin."

"And what would have happened to the daughters?"

"It's happened before."

"Everyone must have breathed a sigh of relief when the son was born. But doesn't that put him under just a little pressure?"

She shrugged. "Mm," she said.

I walked on through richly upholstered room after richly upholstered room and then back down to Scott in the leafy car park.

"How the other half live," I said to him, and eased on to my richly upholstered saddle.

The A-road climbed away from the castle and was quite busy, so I was glad to turn off on to minor roads leading around the outside of the castle grounds. There was a high wall to my left with three men repairing it. The wall went on and on. They could have a long job.

The land changed as I climbed the hills leading away from the Tees valley. The large rape fields were gone. Instead there were hay fields, bullocks and sheep. The lanes were quiet and pleasant, with the uphills mostly gentle before a sudden long descent to the entrance to Hamsterley Forest.

I'd cycled past surprisingly little Forestry Commission woodland on my route, and even here I was barely touching it. A shame really, because there are excellent cycle paths running from the gate south-westwards through the forest. I'd walked here with my family quite recently, and we'd seen other families cycling on the flatter routes and daredevil downhillers racing down the steep routes. We'd stopped for a while at a jump to watch, but the daredevil downhillers spent so long at the top eying up all the options, that in the end we left them to it. I didn't blame them for a bit of caution. I'm not really designed for daredevil downhilling and jumps myself. In the end we thought we'd rather go for a cup of tea.

There was a time when the Forestry Commission saw its role as growing trees, and any other concerns were, well, not their concern. That included public access, leisure pursuits and environmental or ecological issues. Swathes of hillside and valley were cloaked in impenetrable green. Thankfully the organisation has changed completely, and Hamsterley is a good example. Thousands of people come here from the north-eastern cities to cycle or walk and to breathe fresh air.

Yes, I'd have liked to cycle south-west on a nice flat cycleway through the forest. Unfortunately, I was cycling north up a very steep hill through the forest.

I was about to set off when a car purred past me. Not a pussy-cat purr. No, this was a big-cat purr. A tiger, maybe.

"Wow."

Open-topped, with wood and leather. And dark red.

"How's the mid-life crisis?" Scott said.

It really was gorgeous.

"Sorry, what?"

"And does it worry you that you are talking to a bike?"

The car disappeared around a bend.

"Not as much as that you're talking back to me."

Part way up the hill, a forest track slid off to the left, and a fallen tree offered respite. I leaned Scott against it, sat, and ate biscuits.

"Seriously though," he said, "what is the average age and sex of the walkers or cyclists you've met?"

"Hard to say."

"Young? Female?"

"Well, no."

"Middle-aged? Male?"

"Your point?"

"Just developing a hypothesis."

"Well, don't. It will -"

"Stunt my growth?"

"Now you're being silly. But it might get stuck in your chain, and you know you hate that."

Just beyond, the trees ended and the views opened out. Then the road flattened and as it started to descend, I could see the next dale laid out before me: Weardale, with the little village of Wolsingham by the river.

Steep descents are very annoying. They seem such a

waste of all the potential energy (Physics O-level, yes!) that you've just got from cycling uphill. I don't know about the science of it, but a long gentle downhill always seems a better use of the energy. Also a steep descent is almost always accompanied by a steep ascent, and as I braked my way down a twisting road, I could see the steep hill on the other side of Wolsingham, up which I would need to cycle all too soon. Bit depressing really.

Wolsingham was a homely, little place and I sat in the park to munch food and to prepare myself for the next stretch.

That next stretch turned out to be very steep indeed, and I was a touch tired by now (note English understatement please: actually I was shattered). With a couple of view-stops I reached the top to find that the ridge was occupied by the A68 heading directly north and straight to my overnight B&B at Castleside. The plan had been to cross the A68 and take to the lanes, but I could see that would involve losing some of my height all over again. I admitted to myself that I really was very tired, and turned left on to the A68.

That was a mistake. What had seemed a fairly quiet road was not quiet at all. Cars and lorries roared scarily past me and I took a turn off to the right, not really caring now exactly where it went. Instantly all was quiet, and I was on a little lane leading up towards the village of Bruntsfield.

The hill wasn't really big at all. Nothing like I'd done several times that day. But my legs just refused to do it.

"Come on," I said, as they toiled to make any progress.

"What?" Scott said.

"Not you."

It was 5 o'clock and the bike computer said 42 miles, so I'd done farther and faster before today, but I just physically couldn't go on. This was not just a go-slow. My legs were on strike.

I gave in, and collapsed on to a grass verge in the sunshine. I rummaged in my panniers and came out with a bag of nuts, muesli bars and dried fruit. I wolfed it all, plus lots of drink. Then I closed my eyes for ten minutes. Had the verge been a little more comfortable, I might even have slept, but it wasn't, so I didn't.

I checked the map. I was actually nearly there, and there didn't seem to be any more big hills. I sat for a bit longer, then tried again.

"OK, Scott, let's go for it."

"I was alright before."

The hill didn't seem as bad now. Perhaps I needed the refuelling. Anyway, I made it to the village, dropped down over a stream, and then I was suddenly on an absolutely straight road heading north. It was so absolutely straight that it just had to be Roman. The lane itself was just single-track, but the hedges were set well back. I stopped and paced it out to about 12m from hedge to hedge, and then I checked my mileage and cycled until the road stopped at a T-junction. The straight stretch was 1½ miles long.

"What are you doing?" Scott asked.

"Nothing."

At the end of it, my route went off left, but other straight roads came in to meet mine.

"Definitely Roman."

"What?"

"Nothing."

"Heat-stroke."

"Rubbish."

The last bit to the B&B in Castleside had to be on the A68. There was no choice. At the end I took to the pavement. Very wrong of me, I'm sure, but much less scary.

The lady at Castleneuk Guest House was very welcoming. She was absolutely set up for cyclists because I was now crossing the route of the C2C, the increasingly popular Coast To Coast cycle route from Cumbria to Newcastle or Sunderland. She even had a pot of tea ready for me before you

167

could say, "Put your bike in the shed and the tea will be ready before you come in." Which was quite impressive and nearly true.

I had a meal that night in The Smelters Arms. I was on the edge of a very different County Durham to the one I'd been cycling through for most of the day. The one with coal mines, iron and steel. Or at least that used to have coal mines, iron and steel. Consett was just down the road and the terraced houses here made quite a contrast with Raby Castle and its whitewashed estate-farms. This was a different world.

I was starving by now. I looked at the menu and tried to work out which meal would fill me up most. I went for 'toad-in-the-hole'. It was big, but still didn't fill me up. So then I had 'soup-and-a-roll'. That didn't quite do it either. So I went back to my room and ate a 'muesli-bar-and-the-rest-of-the-dried-fruit'. That left a 'single-muesli-bar', and I thoughtfully put it back in my bag.

Captain's log: Day Fourteen
The day's distance: 46.37 miles / 74.19 Km (4th longest so far, with lots of hills; no wonder I'm tired)
The journey so far: 492.66 miles / 788.26 Km (nearly 500 miles; that's a long way)
Average speed: 10.0 mph / 16.0 Kmph (3rd slowest; mm, hills again)
Maximum speed: 38.5 mph / 61.6 Kmph (quickest yet)
Body: absolutely totally banjaxed

10.00pm: went to bed
10.30pm: ate the last muesli bar

Day Fifteen

Target: 31 miles from Castleside to Bellingham, via Hexham and Chesters

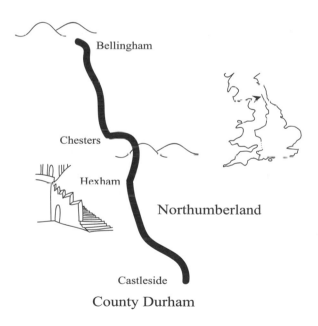

In my original plans for the bike ride, before Man-Flu / black death took hold, I was due to meet my son Richard on this bit of the route. Claire had been going to bring him through to Hexham, and we would do the last four days together. My gap had scuppered that, and instead he would join me for the last two days. I had two more days by myself. Really, I was looking forward to company.

I think Scott was looking forward to company as well.

Cooked breakfast saw me on my way with a very full stomach, and I was glad of the entirely downhill first mile of the day. I was less glad that the next half mile was entirely uphill, nor that all of it was on the A68 again. After four busy miles I was thankful to turn off on to lanes with delicious views across to the Derwent Reservoir down in the valley.

Extraordinarily, I was now in my last county. I was in Northumberland. True, I still had two days until I reached the North Sea, and then two days along the coast. Even so, I had cycled through eleven counties and this was my last. It felt like a milestone.

Curvy roads turned into short straight Roman bursts with wide stretches of grass and yellow gorse and then dry-stone walls either side. A thin cloud was burning off in the sun. It was going to be a hot day again.

An odd-looking bird in a field caught my attention. It was too far off to see well, and it looked a funny shape. Where was a bird-watcher when you needed one? As I set off again, a strange whistling noise came from behind the gorse. *Peep-pe-peep peep-peep*. I slowed, and as I did, a brown-feathered bird flew up. It had a big chest and a long curved beak.

My memory dredged up that it was a curlew.

Peep-peep.

He flew alongside me. *Peep-pe-peep.*

This was amazing. I whistled back at him. Peep-peep.

He kept on beside me. *Peep-pe-peep.*

Hey, I thought, Dr Dolittle or what. Peep-peep.

We'd got up quite a conversation before his wings swept him up and away.

Peep-peep, I whistled.

"It'll be good when Richard joins us," Scott said.

I cycled past the entrance to Slaley Hall Golf Resort, set amongst the large Slaley Forest, and home to an international golf course and hotel. Strange that it should be up amongst the moorland and forest of deepest, darkest County Durham. I admired their choice of location, but I was just a little, well, surprised.

The village of Slaley lay a mile or so beyond, and was a neat little place. I wondered how it and the other tiny villages linked in with the golfing complex that had grown in their midst. Were they grateful for the jobs? Or was it an alien culture over there in the trees?

I hadn't the faintest idea.

It was quiet and peaceful cycling on what was becoming a hot summer's day. The country turned rougher, a mix of woodland and small fields where the farmers kept sheep, cattle and boulders.

There was a sudden dip down to a stone bridge over a stream. A cottage looked over it, with rhododendrons and azaleas blooming in the garden. Oak trees lined the banks. I stopped to look over the parapet, and below me the stream wound gently through rocks and pools. It was simply serene.

There was a plaque on the bridge, and though the stone carving was mostly worn away, there was a transcription: 'God preserve this bridge of lime and stone, 1531'.

It was such a quiet and restful place, that I looked up the name of the river on my map. The river was shown as Devil's Water. Hm.

A big up and down took me into Hexham for 11.30 on the 15 mile mark. The road crept in the back way to the town, down a steep hill past the backs of houses which looked out across Tynedale, the valley of the River South Tyne flowing eastward to the sea at Newcastle.

At the bottom of the hill, I found myself in a busy main street. Opposite, the cars had been banned and the result was a people-friendly shopping area. I pushed Scott through, following signs for The Old Gaol, which turned out to be a very imposing building of great blocks of sandstone. Outside hung a banner saying 'Welcoming Visitors for 600 Years', which was thoughtful.

"Don't think you're chaining me up here," Scott said.

"You don't want to be chained up at the gaol?"

"Actually, no."

"Has anyone ever told you that you're too sensitive?"

"No one who then intended to rest their bottom on my saddle."

I took him back to the shopping area, fixed him in a bike rack and mooched. There seemed to be everything a small town could ask for, including a cinema and a theatre, and I took a liking to the place.

I had a specific target though, Hexham Abbey.

It was dim inside, but shafts of sunlight eased through the windows. The door brought me in next to the Night Stairs, the route by which monastic feet found their way in the dead of night from their dormitory into the church to pray. The steps were well-worn sandstone, and a golden beam of light shone down them.

All of the monastic buildings are gone now, with only the church remaining, and the Night Stairs seemed like a magical reflection of the past.

A medieval monk's hours might have been something like this:

7.30pm	bed
Midnight	**prayer**
1am	back to bed

6am	**prayer**
6.30am	breakfast
7.30am	work
9am	**prayer**
10am	meeting of the 'chapter'
11am	**prayer**
12 noon	dinner
1pm	siesta
2pm	**prayer**
2.30pm	work
4pm	**prayer**
4.30pm	work
6pm	supper
7pm	**prayer**

Which is a lot of **prayer**, and the Night Stairs must have been well-used.

I stood for a while at the top, until a cloud outside dimmed the light and broke the spell. I stepped carefully back down to the stone-flagged floor of the massive church, looking up to the wood-beamed roof high above and around at the great blocks of sandstone making up walls and pillars.

As I'd hoped, the Abbey is like a time-capsule, with stone memories from different eras. The Saxon crypt is put together from Roman stones, while a Roman carving is fixed to the medieval walls, along with 15th century paintings.

The steps down to the crypt were narrow and steep. It was like Ripon, which is not surprising, because this was also the crypt of a St Wilfrid church. The little chapel was small, with now-closed corridors leading off from each side. It's thought that pilgrims would come through those corridors in darkness – there being no candle-niches – into the central chapel where holy relics were illuminated by quiet candles. They would then leave by the narrow staircase into the main body of the church and the sunlight.

It would have been a piece of astonishing theatre.

As I went back up the steps, a silver-haired lady-guide was talking to an American visitor.

"I don't understand the crypt," the American lady was saying. "Where would they put the, y'know…"

"What do you think a crypt is?" the guide asked.

"Well, for bodies?"

"The crypt was for relics, not bodies," the guide said, and I guessed she was answering a question she'd been asked many times before.

The American looked disappointed, but there was no more from the guide; nothing about the corridors, and the darkness and the pure theatre. I wanted to butt in and enthusiastically tell her everything, but I didn't. Too polite and English, I suppose. Sorry.

I had Lunch 1 in the lovely park round the back of the abbey. It was full of lunchers – workers, mums, toddlers – and then investigated the theatre opposite. I recommend the toilets. No idea what the shows are like. But the toilets are good.

Scott was still chained happily in his bike rack in the town centre, sunning himself. I bought more supplies, and we set off.

I got lost cycling out of Hexham.

Twice.

Each time involved cycling up an exceedingly steep hill.

"Are you sure about this?" Scott asked, twice.

The first time, I stopped when I realised I was going south. I asked directions.

The second time, I had the sun on my back and was evidently going north, but there was nobody to ask. I'd crossed the A69 at a scary roundabout and taken a lane up through woods which looked right from my map, but then I'd come to various signposts with villages I didn't recognise. I was not, I thought, discombobulated. No, this time I was lost.

I looked again at the map. It didn't help if I turned it upside down.

It did show the Vallum road running west-east ahead of me: the Roman supply road for Hadrian's wall, now a B-road. As long as I kept on cycling north, I must hit it at some point, and I could then cycle left and would come to Chesters Fort. Easy.

My northerly road kept going up. More and more up, in a now blazing sun. My road was now becoming more farm-track than road, and was still going up. I eventually found myself in a farmyard at the top.

"Ah," I said to Scott.

"Yes?" he said.

"Nothing."

I heard voices in one of the barns.

"Excuse me," I called from the door.

A slightly superior-looking lady looked me up and down, then looked Scott up and down.

"We're lost," I said. "We're trying to get to Chesters."

"Oh," she said, and the slightly superior look disappeared. "Go along the lane until you get to a road. That's the Vallum road. Just go left."

She smiled.

"Thank you," I said.

I eased Scott along the now-flat lane to the Vallum road. "See. Easy."

Almost immediately the dead-straight road dropped long and fast downhill, meaning that the entire climb was a waste of time. Not the best feeling.

Chesters Roman Fort was very hot. A Roman would have felt quite at home. A cyclist didn't.

We parked up and I took an ice cream for a walk around the ruins. Chesters was a cavalry fort on Hadrian's Wall. It was built soon after the Wall itself, marking the boundary of the empire, and keeping out the tribes of the north.

What's left today are the lower levels of some of the dormitories, the commanding officer's house and the bath-house, plus the stumps of the gateways. What I would have liked would have been some reconstructed buildings to show what it would have been like; something big and impressive.

Perhaps it was the heat getting to me, but I took a photo of a sign on a bath-house wall saying 'Hot Room' to cheer myself up.

A guide was trying to enthuse an American coach group, but really it was too hot for them. I sat nearby and pretended not to listen. Gateways… she was saying. Bridge… Bath-house… What it really needed was for the guide to be dressed in full Roman cavalry uniform. With a horse.

The museum could have done with a make-over as well, which was disappointing after, say, Richmond Castle's museum, which also belongs to English Heritage. I did like the model of how Chesters would have looked in its prime. For the first time there was an impression that this was a seriously military place at one time, housing cavalry regiments for nigh on 300 years. But back outside it was just hot again, and I found some shade next to Scott in the car park, had Lunch 2 and re-sun-screened.

I saddled up for the last leg of the day's ride. Up a B-road following the valley of the River North Tyne. At least I was following a valley rather than my usual down one side and up the other, which was a huge improvement.

I wasn't really able to enjoy the woods and the rivers, for taking avoiding action. The traffic was driving altogether too fast, and in greater numbers than I had expected on a road which didn't seem to lead to anywhere other than Bellingham.

The road did receive some nominations though. Three sections of it, recently re-tarmac'd with a totally flat surface, received a nomination for Best Road on Journey. Unfortunately most of the rest received a nomination for Worst Road on Journey, and only went to show why they had started re-surfacing.

The heat and traffic had worn me down by the time I arrived in Bellingham. The bike computer showed a shorter day at 34.39 miles, but it didn't feel like it. Still, Bellingham seemed to have a couple of nice looking pubs, the odd shop and a good few new houses being built. At first sight, it looked a healthy little community. Yet it was tucked away up a little valley, and I wondered what people did for a living up here. The enormous Kielder Forest was just up the road. Perhaps this is where the lumberjacks live. I looked for Canadian-style lumberjack shirts hanging from washing lines, but there didn't seem to be any.

My map suggested the hostel was on the way out of town to the east, and the road – of course – started climbing again alarmingly. I checked with a lady walking her dog and, yes, the YHA had found a site at the top of a hill.

When I found the hostel, it took me back to school days. My school in Bradford on Avon had been housed in a variety of buildings – an imposing Victorian centre-piece in Bath-stone, modern science blocks, and a row of wood-slatted huts which were freezing in the winter, and boiling in the summer. Reputedly, the school huts had been put up during the First World War as a temporary measure, and we'd still been using them in the 1970s.

The hut that is Bellingham YHA looked remarkably similar, except that it had been painted green. It also had shutters at each window, and these had green-and-white triangles painted on them. With green grass all round, and green trees behind, it was all pretty green really.

The hut was long – about twelve windows long, made up of a large-ish section in the middle and two wings.

I leaned Scott against a picnic table by the (green) door and a man came out. He was about forty, with a moustache and a mug of tea. At least he wasn't green.

"Hi," I said. "Are you the warden?"

"There is no warden. I'm a volunteer."

I enquired if he was from the village, but it turned out that he was from the south. Most places in England are south of Bellingham of course – Newcastle, Leeds, Manchester, etc – but I mean really south. Hampshire. Which seemed a long way to come to collect my £10.

It seems that some of the smaller hostels are regularly staffed by volunteers who come and stay for a week. They are long-standing members, who do their own thing during the day, and become temporary wardens for the night in return for a bit of subsistence money.

"What happens," I asked, "if the YHA can't find a volunteer?"

"Someone has to come down from Kielder."

"That would be a pain."

"Did you know this is one of the hostels the YHA are closing?"

"Yes, I read that," I said. "But it's on the Pennine Way. Why would they do that?"

"No idea. Especially when it's staffed by volunteers, so there are no costs really."

I looked closer at the building. The paint was peeling

away alarmingly from the wooden slats.

"It would need some money spent on it, if they were to keep it open. Do many use it?"

"Five tonight."

"Ah. Not enough, I guess."

Separate huts housed a drying room and a bike-shed, plus the volunteer-warden's room. I parked Scott in the bike-shed and followed the mug of tea inside.

In the centre of the hut was a large living area with couches and a TV, plus an ample kitchen. The wings were male and female, with showers / toilets for each. Some of the bunks in the dormitory had already been taken, but I found the quietest corner, parked my panniers underneath, and made up the bed. Again it was the strange elongated sheet-sleeping-bag arrangement, that actually seemed more fitting here in these wooden huts than in the modern surroundings of, say, Coalport YHA.

My companions for the night were already in the lounge. There were three Dutch – a lady and two men. All of them tall, tanned and fit-looking. They were coming to the end of walking the Pennine Way, just a few days away from finishing.

"Are you walking?" one of the men asked me.

"No. Cycling." I felt the need to compete with the Pennine Way. "From Dorset to Berwick."

"Yes. We cycled from Land's End to John O'Groats a few years ago. On a tandem with our camping gear in a trailer."

"Ah."

"Only Cornwall felt hard – getting used to the hills, you know. After that was OK."

"Yes. Yes, it would be."

I had just lost that little competition.

I turned to our other companion so as to regain a little pride. David was a quiet, serious-looking lad, who I guessed was short of his 20th year. Easy.

"Are you walking the Pennine Way as well?"

179

"Yes, well, it's part of my route. I'm actually walking from John O'Groats to Land's End."

"Walking?"

"Yes."

"How long will that take?"

"2½ months."

"2½ months?"

"Yes."

I gave in. "That's great. Brilliant." Damn, I thought.

The Dutch were cooking in the kitchen. Delicious and complex aromas of cooking bacon, tomato and herbs wafted through from the other side of the lounge. I went to the bathroom and washed out a pile of sweaty socks, shirts and underwear. With what I calculated to be impeccable timing, I set off for the pub before the equally complex aromas of my damp underwear also wafted through into the lounge.

I found David, eating by himself.

"Can I join you?" I asked.

He gestured a yes with a full mouth.

"So you must be about half way?"

He finished the mouthful. "I will be in another week."

"And it's just you? Did nobody fancy doing it with you?"

A half-smile. "No. I'd just had enough of work and thought I'd do this."

This was impressive, but a bit sad. "Are you meeting people on the way?"

"My girlfriend met me in Edinburgh and I took a day off."

"Right," I said. "Good."

Back at the hostel, I completed my list of favourite overtakers. The league-leaders, and the relegation contenders:

----

1. Cars carrying bikes (of course).
2. The more mature lady with a curly perm, but not when she couldn't find her glasses.

3. Ladies who wouldn't put themselves into any of the categories at the bottom of the list.

4. Small 'sensible' cars, excluding the red car in Slaithwaite.

5. Flat cap or trilby man.

6. Family cars with a yellow diamond hanging in the back window saying 'Baby on Board', but not a yellow diamond that says 'Grumpy Old Man on Board'. Mental note: must get one for Hugh.

7. The mid-table mass of cars, though the closer to a town centre, the lower they come.

8. Motor bikes – fast and noisy, but at least they are narrow and can fit in the same lane of traffic.

9. Estate car drivers who used to have a small fast car (see below).

10. Drivers of small fast cars who suddenly appear at your shoulder and overtake **no matter what the oncoming traffic.**

11. Lorries; now these are hard to categorise because some are well-driven and some badly; all are scary.

12. Coaches – the older, the worse.

13. Four-wheel-drive cars; these drivers do actually own the road – it's in the Highway Code somewhere, I'm sure

14 White van man, and the sub-category of white van man who can't afford a proper-size white van and hasn't forgiven the world for that and drives too close behind and then overtakes when a lorry is coming the other way and "I've got your number you - **B something**. Again. **And a ... 7**. Or a 6. I think. Well, **it had a B in it**."

15. That red car in Slaithwaite. Oh, yes.

I felt better for that.

Captain's log: Day Fifteen
The day's distance: 34.39 miles / 55.02 Km
The journey so far: 527.05 miles / 843.28 Km
Average speed: 11.1 mph / 17.76 Kmph
Maximum speed: 35.5 mph / 56.8 Kmph

David, though. There was a girlfriend. I was pleased.
I sincerely hoped she was patient.

Day Sixteen

Target: 35 miles from Bellingham to Alnmouth, via Rothbury, Brinkburn Priory and Alnwick

The next morning, David was ready to go by 8 o'clock. On his back he had a huge rucksack with a tent strapped on top.

The unattached of the tall Dutch men said to him, "It's going to be hhot again today," in that guttural Dutch way that I quite like, emphasising the 'h's.

David said, "Yes," and headed for the door. I'd like to say he staggered under what must have been a very heavy weight, but he didn't. He'd been carrying it for over a month.

"Have a good day," I said.

"I will."

And he was gone.

"Hhe's young, isn't hhe? To do that by hhimself."

"Yes," I said. "Did you know he has a girlfriend?"

"Good."

"Yes. I thought that."

I would bump into the Dutchman again in a few days time, at Berwick station. I felt sorry for him there. He was by himself, waiting for a train, after which he would be waiting for a flight to Holland, a bit of an anti-climactic end to an epic walk. You needed, I thought, somebody to share an ending with. Richard would be joining me that evening for the last two days, and that was perfect.

In the mean time, I had Scott.

I suppose.

I brought him out of the bike shed into the sunshine, leaned him on a picnic bench again, and collected my mostly-dry underwear from the drying room, laying it out to air on the table by Scott.

"Erm," he said, "you couldn't just move me upwind, could you?"

I hung the socks from his handlebars and went to have breakfast.

I'd enjoyed staying in YHA hostels. The B&Bs were more comfortable and private. But you didn't really talk to anybody, and you couldn't wash your clothes and leave them in a drying room overnight. At hostels, people talked, and my socks would smell a little bit better.

The three Dutch were off before me, and I wished their football team a bad World Cup. They cheerfully predicted likewise for England, whose first match was the following day at 2 o'clock. I would have to make arrangements to see that. But first I had to get to Alnmouth.

My friend with the moustache and the mug of tea appeared, and I asked him directions. Easy, apparently. My route coincided for a while with NCN Route 68 – the Pennine Cycleway. Then I would head off to the coast. Hills in the morning. Flatter in the afternoon. Fine.

The hostel was on the right road, so I cycled straight out of town, then through the hamlets of West and East Woodburn, and up on to the tops.

It was just magnificent. I was on lanes and farm tracks rising and falling with the land. The Cheviot Hills were off to the left, the Simonside hills to the right. It was easily the quietest part of the journey so far. Just the occasional car to a farm; the odd farmer repairing a dry-stone wall; and sheep. Not namby-pamby southern sheep, but rough, tough northerners, with black faces, curly horns, and un-shorn wool hanging off them. Growing-up lambs jolted viciously at their teats.

There were also bullocks in the fields. Some were enormous, chunky beasts, while others were this year's calves, big-eyed and easily scared by an unexpected bike. Mostly they were a common brown or black, but some had a black front, a black behind, and a broad white stripe down the middle. It was like a children's book where you can turn part of the page to make unlikely farm animals. Turn the page again, and it would have a pink bum.

After a short climb on an A-road, my route dropped into the small village of Elsdon. Sensible stone-built houses encircled a vast village green with a church in the middle. From the edge of the village I could see a stone tower at the top of the village, but from the bottom of the sloping green, the tower disappeared.

I cycled up to where it had seemed to be. Trees screened the spot, but there was a gate with a notice attached, giving permission to walk up the drive to see the Elsdon's very own pele tower.

Pele towers were built to defend villagers against cross-border raiders – reivers – who for centuries attacked, stole cattle, kidnapped and murdered across this whole border region. Most pele towers have long been abandoned. With their thick walls and tiny windows, they are not ideal for modern living. This one, though, was very much not abandoned.

Elsdon's pele tower is four storeys high, square-built and strong, of golden rough-cut stone blocks. As it was in the 14th century, it would have been a powerful defensive structure, with arrow-slits instead of windows. Now, a large arched window illuminates the ground floor, and a Victorian-looking extension has the makings of a comfortable 19th century rectory. I loved it.

It was half past ten, warm and sunny, and I leaned myself against a wall looking down over the green and the church, and ate biscuits. Behind me, someone was mowing the pele tower's lawn. This was good.

I wandered into the church, which was also 14th century. Must have been a good century for Elsdon folk. Perhaps they'd stolen plenty of cattle from the Scots just across the border and sold them down at Richmond's market square.

The church was calm and peaceful; stone-walled and wood-pewed. Cool against the heat outside. I sat in a pew and read some of the church's history in a booklet. When the church had been renovated, three horse skulls had been found built into a wall, the most likely explanation being some sort of pagan ritual. I wondered what the Rector in his pele-tower rectory up the hill must have thought.

Outside, Scott was waiting patiently. I cycled down the slope, and found two cyclists coming the other way. A couple. Tall. Dutch.

They asked if I could recommend anywhere not too hilly to cycle. I looked at the hills all around me, and I looked at the map.

"Erm, no," I said. I showed them my map, and really, there were no flat roads at all.

"That's OK," the man said. "We cycle."

And they did. I watched them go and wondered just how two Dutch people with bikes had managed to find themselves in the Pennines and surprised by there being hills, all at the same time.

As I climbed my road out of Elsdon on to moorland, red flags were being flown to the left. I was on the edge of Otterburn army camp, and presumably the red flags meant that there were weapons being fired across there.

"Go quicker, Scott," I said.

As the red flags passed, the road started to drop. The moorland became softer and the sheep whiter and woollier. Soon I was following a river down into a valley. Bluebells lined the banks of the road, and the views opened out to show fields bounded by white hawthorn-bush hedges rather than by dry-stone walls. There were certainly ups to cycle, but now they were outnumbered by the downs. I was coming out of the Pennines.

The wind got up and blew from the east, which was the way I was cycling. With that and the heat, the last few miles into Rothbury felt hard. By the time I arrived in the busy market town at 12 o'clock, my legs were aching. 23 miles that morning, I noted, and I needed a break.

I chained Scott to a bench under a tree and bought a (cold) pasty at a baker's. (Cold! Who sells cold pasties?) As I ate, it occurred to me that if I had done 23 miles that morning, my target distance of 35 miles might be a bit of an under-estimate. I decided against telling Scott.

Rothbury was a pretty enough place, with trees and a grassy bank by the road, and real shops beyond. It seemed to be full of tourists, but they did appear to be tourists unsure of what there was to do in Rothbury. I had a look in the visitor centre, which I'm sure is where many of the tourists headed, but it wasn't, shall we say, big. Then I had a look in the church. And then I went back and sat on the bench next to Scott.

"I think it might be more than 35 miles today," I told Scott. Well, it was conversation.

Scott, however, said nothing, though the leather-clad motor-biker at the other end of the bench gave me a funny look.

I decided it was time to go.

Purple rhododendron bushes lined the road out of town, and I knew I must be cycling past Cragside.

Cragside was the house on the hill above me, built in the 19th century by the inventor and industrial magnate, Lord Armstrong. At his Cragside mansion, Armstrong developed hydro-electric power for domestic use and also incorporated hot and cold running water, central heating, telephones, fire alarms and a lift. A man ahead of his time.

I'd been before, years ago, and my major memory was not of those wonders, but of a truly enormous marble fireplace. If memory serves, it had been so big and so heavy, that they'd had to rest it on bedrock and build the house around it.

Beyond the rhododendrons, the Armstrong alms houses and the Armstrong rugby ground, the road led down the valley of the river Coquet – Coquetdale, the map said, which has a nice ring to it.

It was just a few easy-ish miles before a sign for my next stop – Brinkburn Priory. I turned into the little lane, left Scott in an empty car park, and walked on down the hill through the woods.

Just in front of the Priory was a little English Heritage hut. I peered around in search of a tea-room, but there was none. Even the toilets were Portaloos around the back. Which is a pity, because English Heritage could make more of the place.

The early history of Brinkburn Priory is like many medieval abbeys.

1. Monks.
2. Henry VIII.
3. Dissolution.
4. Ruin.
5. Manor house built next door with stone from the ruins.

But from then on there is a change. In the 19th century, the owners of the manor house developed a fascination with the ruins. They brought in historians and professionals, and set about rebuilding the abbey church as closely as they could to the original.

I went in through a fabulous Norman doorway, round-arched and decorated with chevrons. Inside, the darkness was cut by shafts of light from colour-filled stained glass windows high above. There were no pews, of course, because this was a re-creation of a medieval church, not a used building. I pottered around, down the side-aisle, into the chapels, and up to the altar.

It was quiet. Too quiet.

By which I mean that there weren't enough visitors. Some did appear while I was there, but I do think a little tea shop and an exhibition might be a good plan.

Next to the church, the manor house is still there, but only just. Ironically, it is the manor house which is now partly ruined, while the church is standing tall and complete.

Some of the house can be walked through. Many of the walls are tumbling, and behind one stretch of plaster-less wall can be seen the remains of some of the monastic buildings. Perhaps part of a cloister, or a refectory, which had become an internal wall of the manor house.

It must have been a lovely home in its time, with romantic ruins on one side, and a river bound by woods on the other. I wondered how it had fallen into decay like this. The manor was a sad place now.

I wandered back to the English Heritage hut, where I still couldn't buy a cup of tea.

The B-road dropped further down the valley and deposited me on to the A697, a straight stretch up an incline, which looked a bit busy with cars and lorries for comfort. However, my map showed a section of the old road just opposite, which was not straight, not busy and went more gently uphill. I thankfully took that, and it was really very peaceful until the shooting started.

I'd heard shotguns once or twice on my journey. You do in the countryside. So for the first thirty seconds or so of shooting, I paid no attention. But it just kept on going. I stopped and looked through some trees downhill towards a small wood, but could see nothing to suggest what was going on. My route led me back to the main road and then sharp right, so that I was cycling two sides of a square. All that time, the shooting went on. Ten minutes. Twenty minutes. Then I took a sharp left towards Swarland village, and the noise slowly ebbed into the distance. I couldn't understand it. Had there been a massacre of everything fluffy and furry within the wood? Or was it a small invasion?

As I cycled through Swarland, a house had two military vehicles outside. Another actually had a tank. Small invasion, then, I thought, and I pedalled a touch faster.

Newton-on-the-Moor must presumably have been a New Town on a Moor at one stage, but this felt nothing like the Pennine moorland I'd come down from that morning. This was lowland farming country, basking gently in the summer sun.

Just beyond Newton, I came to the dual-carriageway of the A1. Not a good place to be for a bike. I only had to cross it, not cycle on it, but even so, I took about ten minutes to get to the far side as lorries and cars hurtled past. It was late Friday afternoon, and they obviously had places to be.

The wind was getting stronger now, and it wasn't a warm wind. Strangely, in the sunshine, I was getting chilly. I cycled the ups and downs, not serious ones, northwards towards Alnwick, and the reason for the chilliness became clear. All along the horizon on my right, a dark sea-mist was blanketing the coast. Where I was, the sun was shining. In Warkworth and Alnmouth on the coast, it would be thick mist and cold, and that was where the wind was coming from. Today was meant to be me reaching the North Sea, but when I got there, I might not see anything at all.

The road into Alnwick led through the gatehouse of the old town walls, a huge construction of sandstone blocks, with just room for a single line of traffic. The other side, into the town centre, had smart brick-set pavements, busy shops and enticing cafés. The centre itself was a cobbled market square, pedestrianised and surrounded by original buildings, some sensible and straight-faced, others columned and fancy. Around the square had been set benches, and I perched myself on one to decide just how much I liked Alnwick. Quite a lot, I thought. Apparently I'm not alone in that; Country Life magazine has voted Alnwick the best town in the country to live in.

What I didn't have time for, partly because I was due to meet Richard and Claire at Alnmouth down on the coast very soon, and partly because it was now closed, was the castle. I cycled around to look at the astonishing castle walls and gatehouse, with their blackened stone statues standing guard on the battlements, and the Percy lion above the gateway. If Middleham and Raby Castles had been seats of power in North Yorkshire and Durham, Alnwick was the seat of power in Northumberland. Alnwick was the home of the Percy family.

Neville and Percy were the two great families of the north of England, dominating the land and the politics for generations. A significant difference was that the Nevilles over-reached themselves in the time of Elizabeth I and were brought to their knees. The Percy Earls and Dukes of Northumberland might have pushed things to the limit once or twice, but were still here in the time of Elizabeth II. The castle has been here for at least 900 years, and the Percy family for about 700 of them.

These days the family use something other than brute force to hold on to their home. They seem to know the value of the great new industry of England – the leisure industry. Visits to the castle have been boosted by the shooting of films and TV programs here. The castle is not just home to the Duke, but also to Harry Potter.

The road to Alnmouth wasn't brilliant. Narrow at times and busy with going-home-at-Friday-tea-time traffic. But it wasn't far, and then I was in the tiny and quaint village, with a little main street that only led to one place – the sea. What's more, the sea was there, not covered by mist, but blue and gorgeous beyond grassy sand-dunes and a creamy beach. In the distance a white sail leaned into the breeze.

"Scott," I said. "Photo." I leaned him against an information board on a stone plinth, sat myself on a bench, and said, "Smile."

"I don't think that's my best side."

This was exciting. My first sea since Portland. "Now me."

I steadied the camera on the bench, set the timer, and sprinted to Scott. I did my best **Heroic Explorer Discovers New Sea**, and waited. Unfortunately I turned back to the camera too soon, and the **Heroic Explorer Discovers New Sea** was more **Heroic Explorer Looks Slightly Blurred**.

"Again," I said to Scott.

"Oh dear Lord," he said.

By the time Claire and Richard appeared, I was happy.

Scott was not, but then, be honest, how many times have you seen a mountain bike *really* happy?

There were hugs along the sea-front of Alnmouth. It was so good to see them.

The guest house was just around the corner and we walked happily along.

Beryl was a bustling lady of mature years. She showed us into a chintzy room, with pink cushion covers and roses on the wallpaper, and pointed out the en-suite bathroom, the TV and the tea-and-coffee-making-facilities, just in case we couldn't see them.

Everything was clean and dainty, and I almost immediately discarded the idea of bringing Scott in to clean his chain on newspaper on the bedroom floor.

"Dinner is at seven," Beryl said, twitching to be some-where else doing important things. "I'll come back with your menus."

We made tea and coffee from the tea-and-coffee-making-facilities, and put on the TV. It was the World Cup, which was fine by two of us.

"This is not quite what I expected," Claire said.

"It's not really what I expected either."

"How much was it?"

"Fifty pounds. Cheaper than anywhere else that had space. And that includes dinner. *Inexpensive and spotless*, I'd say."

We stowed both bikes behind the garage and brought in Richard's panniers.

Beryl poked her head in with the three-course dinner menu and also the cooked breakfast menu. This was a tight ship. Nothing was to be left to chance. Efficiency was all.

"This is amazing value," Claire said, and it was at this moment that it occurred to me that I might have got the price wrong.

Claire had to leave. She'd have liked to do these last two days with us. I'd have liked her to as well, but there were all sorts of other things happening, and the timing wasn't right. She'd do it another time. We'd do it another time.

The dining room had about a dozen tables, all covered with pristine white table cloths bearing folded napkins and a little bunch of flowers. Classical music played gently in the background.

Each seat was labelled with a name. We found *Mike* and *Richard* in the corner near the window, and watched as the other tables filled up. Each new couple seemed older than the last, until finally there was a sea of grey hair. Richard must have had at least fifty years on any other diner apart from me, though the average was more like sixty. I was starting to feel like we had been caught up in an 'outing', and I could see Richard was wishing we hadn't been.

As the two waitresses cleared away dessert dishes, the music was switched off, a spoon was knocked on a glass, and everyone looked up.

"Now," Beryl was saying, "one of you has tried to keep something from me."

Silence.

Oh God, what have I done?

"Bob."

Thank you, Lord.

The balding, slight man next to our table cringed and reddened. His wife put a supportive hand on his arm.

"Bob," Beryl went on, "is seventy today, and I want us all to sing Happy Birthday." She took a deep breath. "**Happy Birthday To You, Happy-**"

Poor Bob was sunk as low in his seat as he could.

"**-Birthday To You-**"

I heard my own voice join in, and gradually everyone in the room was singing.

"**-Happy Birthday Dear-**"

Except Richard.

"**-Bo-ob-**"

Richard was cringing almost as low as Bob. He looked across at me with eyes that implored me to get him out of this room.

"**-Happy Birthday To You,**" I sang.

With gusto.

Oh what fun we had.

Captain's log: Day Sixteen
The day's distance: 48.61 miles / 77.78 Km
The journey so far: 575.66 miles / 921.06 Km
Average speed: 10.7 mph / 17.12 Kmph
Maximum speed: 33.5 mph / 53.6 Kmph

Back in our room, Richard said, "I'm going to tell her it's your birthday at breakfast."

I said, "I'm going to tell her we're twins."

Day Seventeen

Target: 34 miles from Alnmouth to Fenwick, via Seahouses and Bamburgh

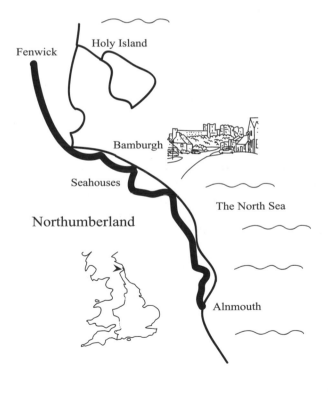

Fenwick

Holy Island

Bamburgh

Seahouses

Northumberland

The North Sea

Alnmouth

The BBC weather man was pointing at a map covered in big yellow suns. "It's going to be 30° for most of the country today, so don't do anything energetic."

I opened the curtains. It was cold and grey with a strong wind blowing, and I expressed my heartfelt thanks to the BBC for their predictive skills and also their sound advice, with only a small reference to the value of the TV licence fee.

Breakfast was almost as bizarre as dinner. All the cooked breakfasts were delivered by name to each table to the exact order of the previous evening. Well, almost exact. We had nearly finished when a waitress with a soft Irish lilt to her voice appeared at our table with two sausages on a plate. She was plainly very nervous.

"Are you missing your sausages?" she said.

"Er, no."

"Only, we've these left over. So someone must have ordered them and not got them."

"Not us, I'm afraid."

She worked her way around every table, finally admitting defeat, and her shoulders slumped as she left to tell Beryl that the system had crashed horribly, and that two cold sausages were unclaimed. Alnmouth's unemployment rate might have doubled that morning.

The lady at the table by the window leaned across to me. "We're only here for two nights. Any more and I'd go stir crazy."

"We're only here for one night. We go today."

"Oh," she said, and there was real envy in her eyes.

Bob and his wife were keeping a low profile at the table behind us. "Last year," Bob said, "the family organised a surprise party for me. I couldn't take another one, so we thought we'd come up here out of the way."

His wife said, "I'm afraid I mentioned it to one of the other guests yesterday. She must have told Beryl. It's all my fault."

I looked around conspiratorially. "I'm thinking of organising an escape committee."

"Count us in," Bob said.

We packed up to leave, and I interrupted Beryl's comings and goings from the dining room to ask for the bill. I did so with a little trepidation now. Had I misheard the £50 she had said on the phone?

"I think I said £50, didn't I?" she said.

"Yes." What a relief.

"So, £50 each is £100, please."

Each.

£50 each.

"Yes, of course. Um, can I give you a cheque?"

Each!

So, easily the most expensive overnight on the trip. Still at least we had the sing-song the night before.

Expensive and bizarre.

I phoned the B&B we were to stay in that night.

"Um, just checking that we are still OK to stay tonight?"

"Yes, of course."

"And it was £60?"

"Yes."

"For both of us?"

"Yes."

"Not each?"

"No."

I breathed again.

"And, well, the football is due to start at 2 o'clock. The England match. I wasn't sure whether to make for a pub to watch it or to come straight there. Would you be in?"

"You're welcome to watch it here."

Richard and I consulted. To get there by 2 o'clock would mean some fairly fast riding. I'd reckoned on 35 miles for today along National Cycle Network 1, which was here called the Coast and Castles Route. Richard was a pretty fit

14-year-old, but he hadn't done the distances I had over the last few weeks. He might be struggling by the end.

"What would you rather?" I asked. "Go for it, with very few breaks, and watch it in comfort? Or take our time, and find a pub somewhere along the way to watch it?"

"Go for it?"

"Are you sure?"

"Yes."

We went for it. We were on the coast now, with only a few hills, but the very first of them saw me struggling to keep up with Richard. I had cycled 48.61 miles the day before, and my leg muscles were reminding me of that.

"I think," I said, breathing heavily, "we should take it easy on the hills. Long way to go."

For the next few miles the route ducked away from the sea, then back to it, away again, and back to it, along quiet country lanes. On either side were fluffy sheep, rape fields or grain. All very pleasantly rural, with glimpses of the sea across fields or through hedges. Boulmer was quiet. Longhoughton was quiet. It was lovely. Even the sun came out, although the wind stayed with us and it wasn't warm.

"I'm a bit worried that we shouldn't be doing exercise in these temperatures," I said. "The BBC did warn us."

"Shall we stop?"

"Mm, in a bit, perhaps."

Outside Longhoughton a buzzing noise caught up with us. It grew louder and I became convinced that a pack of rabid lawnmowers was on our tail. A dozen scooters overtook. Neeamm. Neeamm. Probably Alnmouth's Mods. Neeamm.

"Saturday afternoon fight in Bamburgh, do you think?"

"Probably."

"Don't worry, Scott," I said.

"Scott?"

"My bike. Look. On the side. Scott."

"Oh."

"We're making good time, I think."

At the little hamlet of Dunstan, the NCN1 route took us off-road. A slow-riding rubbly farm-track ran parallel with the coast, giving us distant views of the romantically-placed Dunstanburgh Castle ruined on a headland. Two towers still stood against the sky, the land flat between them. Two incisor teeth standing alone in an old jaw-bone of land.

We found our way into Embleton and back to the B-road, where I consulted the map. If we stuck to the B-road, rather than stay on the NCN1, we could probably cut a mile or two off our route. It was approaching mid-morning, and we still had 22 miles or so to go.

"Rich. Your choice. Use the B-road and make sure we get there in time for the football? Or do this ride properly by sticking to the Coast and Castles route?"

The B-road traffic turned out to be very light, and we pedalled straight and fast. The few cars tended to have England flags fluttering from both sides. The excitement was growing.

I kept looking at my watch. We'd be OK. Not early, maybe, but OK.

The road kept us away from the sea for a few miles, before a right-angle turn headed us straight into Beadnell on the 19 mile mark. I'd thought we would stop at Beadnell, but really there was not much to keep us there. A caravan park, a newsagent and a fish-and-chip shop. Hardly anyone about. We sat on a bench in the sun to polish off a pack of dried fruit.

"Do you realise your bike has a name as well?"

"No."

"Look. On the side."

He read, "ROCK SE. Roxie?"

"Well…"

"No."

"Rock?"

"OK."

I did the introductions. "Scott. Rock. Rock. Scott."

Richard was inspecting me in an unusual manner.

"I've been by myself quite a while now," I said.

Seahouses was very different to Beadnell. With the England match a matter of hours away, cars bearing flags of St George were queued down the main street. Exhaust fumes competed with the smells of sticky lollies and ice-creams in little hands, and of cans of lager in bigger hands.

"Do you want to wait with the bikes, Rich, and I'll get sandwiches," I said.

Easier said than done. The shops were heaving. A group of beer-bellied England fans in their red and white shirts were queuing to get Buy-One-Get-One-Free 6-packs of beer and multi-packs of crisps.

When I finally reached the front of the check-out queue, I was starting to panic. Time was moving on. The fans here might not have far to carry their cans, but Richard and I had a good few miles to go.

I stuffed the sandwiches in a pannier, and we inched down the main street through the traffic, until at the harbour we were able to head out of town and along the coast road towards Bamburgh.

The road was straight and fast, and the wind was behind us. Astonishing, but true. We raced along.

Bamburgh Castle appeared ahead of us, squatting on a rock. At first it didn't look as large as I remembered, but we were still some way off. As we got closer, the castle grew, and it became clear that this was another massive fortress, sitting astride a giant rock and dominating the otherwise flat coast.

The volcanic mound on which the castle sits has been home to fortifications forever. Celts, Anglo-Saxons and Normans all built here and fought here. Vikings and Scots raided here. Even Warwick the Kingmaker made time to come north to besiege the castle for nine months during the

Wars of the Roses.

After that, the castle was left to fall into ruin, until another of the characters I had met on my journey stepped in. Lord Armstrong, industrialist, engineer, and owner of Cragside at Rothbury, bought the remains of the once-mighty castle. He was 80 when he started the restoration, which is ambitious. His family continued the work, and still own Bamburgh.

Now that would be some place to live.

Richard and I cycled up the sharp little slope to the car park, and chained Scott and Rock to a fence next to the castle gateway. High walls of pink sandstone blocks loomed above us, some of it worn and weathered, other stretches flat and newer. Arched windows looked out along the perfect beaches under a grey sky.

We dropped down into the dry moat to try to get out of the chilly wind and found ourselves looking up at a sea of ivy covering the rock-face and stretching up to the base of the walls.

As a 'get-out-of-the-wind' spot, it left something to be desired. As a 'wow-look-at-that-castle-up-there' spot, it was perfect, and we got out our lunch.

We didn't have long though. It was after 12 o'clock. Less than two hours to go.

"Have you finished your sandwich, Rich?"

"Bleugh."

"I'll take that as a yes."

We unchained our bikes and sped down the steep hill into the village, where we made an emergency stop at the public toilets. The view back towards the castle was fabulous. Bamburgh really must be one of the most picturesque places in England. The castle makes such a spectacular backdrop to the olde-worlde village with its little cottages, gas-lamp-type street-lights and grass lawns.

The map showed about ten miles left, but ten hilly miles. The first of them was a long pull up to a ridge. We'd cycled

over twenty miles at a fast pace with only brief breaks, and it was starting to show. Richard was slowing down. He made it though, and we raced down the far side and then past Waren Mill on the Budle Bay estuary. Beyond it, we rejoined the NCN1 route, with its little blue signposts that should lead us right to our B&B in Fenwick, just short of Holy Island.

On the far side of the A1 a long, long hill took us up into the village of Belford. That was hard. But then we were on what must have been the old A1, and it was straight and downhill long enough to rejuvenate the legs a little for the last stretch to Fenwick.

Those last few miles seemed to go on for ever and Richard's legs were hurting before we turned into the village. It was 1.50pm. We had made it.

The guest house was beautiful, with steps leading up through a little paved garden to stone-built walls and mullioned windows. Inside there were pointy-arched doors, wooden beams and a wide-screen TV. We had arrived in heaven just in time for the football.

This was not as expensive as the previous night, of course, but it was a trifle more than I had planned on spending. A lot more than some of the roofs had cost that had kept the rain off. So I think I can describe it as, say, '*moderately priced for a B&B and totally wonderful*'. It doesn't have the same ring as *'expensive but spotless'*, but there's thought there.

I would here like to apologise to our hostess for not chatting fulsomely on the doorstep, but, well, the football was on.

England won. One – nil.

So that was good.

We retired to our room in a good frame of mind to alternately shower and, well why not, to watch the next World Cup match. We were still in heaven.

When the second match finished, we went to find our hostess.

"Is there a pub in the village where we can eat?"

"No, I'm afraid not. There's one a couple of miles away. We could drive you if you like, but we have to go out later, so you might have to walk back."

"Right."

"It's downhill on the way there, but uphill back."

"Ah."

"Or you could cycle, of course."

We abruptly left heaven.

Captain's log: Day Seventeen
The day's distance: 35.29 miles / 56.46 Km
The journey so far: 610.95 miles / 977.52 Km
(nearly 1,000 kilometres - seems a lot)
Average speed: 12.4 mph / 19.84 Kmph
(fastest yet; maybe something to do with a football match?)
Maximum speed: 33.5 mph / 53.6 Kmph

The two miles downhill were OK.

The food in the pub was not bad.

The third football match of the day on the pub's TV was alright.

But I can't say that either of us really enjoyed the two miles continuous uphill on the way back.

Day Eighteen

Target: 33 miles from Fenwick to the Scottish border, via Holy Island and Berwick-upon-Tweed

Russia

Scotland

Berwick-upon-Tweed

Germany

The border

Northumberland

Holy Island

Fenwick

Today was always going to be a day of mixed emotions. It was the last day of the ride. All being well, I would be at the Scottish border during the afternoon and then I'd be going home. Home was good. But also, the journey would end, and as we packed up that morning, I wasn't sure how I felt about that.

Our hostess appeared with two plates.

"The full English," she said.

I almost said, "Yes, it has been really." But I might have been misunderstood.

"Thank you. Lovely."

The breakfast was truly enormous. We were both glad that we were repeating the two miles downhill from last night. Then we were going to make a detour. Richard and I were going to Holy Island.

We negotiated the A1 by the pub. A short sharp uphill, a descent through trees, and we were on the coast. Straight ahead, beyond rough grass laced with tiny pink flowers, was the causeway to Holy Island.

We stopped to take in the view. Surprisingly far away, the main island rose against the haze of a steel sea and a sky that couldn't quite decide to let the sun past the clouds. It was still a two-shirt cycling day. We could maybe guess at a village on the far right of the island, with grey fingers of height that might be the abbey. The road ahead was absolutely flat and very inviting.

"Shall we go for it?" I said.

Richard, in his bright red England shirt, grinned. "Yeh."

We raced for about half a mile into a strong wind, legs pumping, hearts beating wildly, before – for me at least – enough was enough.

"Hey, Rich," I shouted, slowing. "This is too much like hard work."

He still looked fresh. "OK," he said.

I'd already accepted that he could overtake me running

up hills in the Lake District. I'd already accepted that on a steep hill on a training ride, he'd be waiting at the top.

"Don't rub it in," I said.

"What?" Pretended innocence.

"The tortoise," I said, "and the hare." I would still win on endurance, but that was only a matter of time.

I tortoised on; the hare waited for me.

The tide was out. Either side of the tarmac'd causeway, mudflats stretched away into the distance. Here and there, pools of sea-water remained, waiting for the next tide to reclaim ownership. It was odd to think that where we were cycling would be under deep water in just a few hours.

Wind-blown sand started to appear on the road, and then on our right were drifts of the pretty pink flowers amongst stubby grass. The road must have imperceptibly risen. We were on the island. To our left, sand-dunes appeared, patches of long spiky grass holding them in place.

The road turned slightly more south, still dead flat and straight, but now further into the wind, and my legs could feel that they were putting in some work.

The village came closer and we passed bungalows and little houses before we found ourselves in the old village square. Here stood small thick-walled cottages, a hotel and a pub. The sun came out, and all was right with the world.

We walked through towards the ruined Priory, originally founded by monks from Scotland's Island of Iona led by a monk by the name of Aidan. He had been invited by the Anglo-Saxon King of Northumbria to preach to the pagan people of the Kingdom, and he based himself right here on what was then known as Lindisfarne. It was this moment, 635AD that could be said to be the start of the Christianising of England.

A successor of Aidan, Cuthbert, was renowned for healing and for miracles. After Cuthbert died, it became known that his body hadn't decayed. Pilgrims began to flock to the 'holy island'.

By the end of the 8th century, England was increasingly wealthy, and much of that wealth was in monasteries like Lindisfarne's, temptingly close to the sea.

'*There were exceptional flashes of lightning, and fiery dragons were seen flying through the air*," a chronicler wrote a hundred years on. "*A great famine soon followed these signs; and a little after that the harrying of the heathen miserably destroyed God's church in Lindisfarne by rapine and slaughter.*'

I'd stood on Portland Beach in the same place that the first Viking raid on Anglo-Saxon England had taken place. Now, on my last day, I was at the site of the second. Holy Island and Portland Beach were book-ends, a touch of symmetry at either end of my book-shelf of a bike-ride.

Nothing at all is left of the Anglo Saxon monastery, but the Norman ruins that Richard and I found are romantic and graceful enough: the broken walls and columns; the high arch no longer supporting a roof; the lawn where stone and tile would have carried monks' sandaled feet. Tourists were wandering in the sunshine, a young couple playing with their toddler. We'd played with our kids amongst a few National Trust or English Heritage ruins in our time. This was perfect.

I took a photo of Richard sitting on the plinth of a statue of St Aidan. Richard in his England top, St Aidan ten foot high and made of sandstone. Just a little incongruous.

"Stop taking photos of me."

"No."

The morning was wearing on, and we cycled across the island towards Lindisfarne Castle. The tourists had started to arrive in numbers, all walking towards the castle. We weaved in and out of German, Dutch, American and occasional English accents, parking the bikes at the gate leading up to the castle itself.

It was built as a fortress to defend England against

Scottish invasion shortly before a Scottish King was invited to be King of England. Timing. That's what you need.

The castle wasn't big. This was no Bamburgh or Alnwick, but a castle in miniature, filling every square inch of a rocky point at the southern tip of the island.

A wall ran around the highest part of the hill, with a small tower poking out at the top, from where visitors watched us walking up the cobbled slope.

The entrance was a funny little cabin, but what followed inside was wonderful. The castle had become a ruin through the centuries, only for the editor of Country Life magazine to invite architect Edwin Lutyens to create an 'ideal home'. Lutyens's ideal home was the inside of a Dutch painting, and in 1903, that's what he made here. Walking around it was like being inside a Rembrandt or a Vermeer. There was the interplay of dark and light, the heavy wooden furniture, and the paintings. A lady-guide of vintage years was in one of the rooms. I had half expected a girl with a pearl earring, but no.

"A beautiful place," I said.

"Isn't it?"

"Do you live on the island?"

"No. We come up here for a few weeks each summer as volunteers."

"Oh, right."

"The National Trust let us have a holiday cottage. We have to pay, but it's not too much."

"You must really enjoy doing this?"

"Oh yes. Every day someone has a question we can't answer and we have to find out. My husband's in the next room. This is our third year."

A group of visitors arrived. In the narrow confines of corridors and small rooms, it started to feel crowded. Lutyens's ideal home probably didn't include tourists, and with the peace and quiet gone, we made our way back to the bikes.

The wind was behind us on the causeway as we cycled off the island.

We hared along.

When I called for a halt it was not to get my breath but to climb the white-painted wooden stairs of the little refuge part way across the causeway. It was about 15 feet above the road, a little wooden box of a room. I wondered what it would feel like to have misjudged the tide and to end up spending a few hours here, while the sea swirled underneath you. Precarious, I imagine.

At the far side, I was looking out for what was meant to be a new part of NCN1, following the coast rather than the country lanes inland. I almost missed it, since there was a dirty-great yellow digger in the way. The dirty-great yellow digger was in fact still working on it.

The new route was great fun, sometimes grass, sometimes track, and was still lumpy and humpy, maybe waiting to be tamped down. We were cycling parallel to the dunes with, now and then, a sight of the sea through grass and sand.

"Rich, this is fantastic," I shouted, bumping over hillocks. "Glad we've got mountain bikes."

Richard grinned back at me, obviously enjoying himself. "It's brilliant."

I lurched almost to a stop in a little sand trap where the covering grass had been worn away. "Whoa."

"Are you OK?"

"Fine. Yes."

"Bet this is tricky in the rain."

He was quite right, as well – doing this on a road bike in the sort of rain I'd been in would have been desperate.

We stopped to refuel where the cycle route turned back into road. Chocolate biscuits. I think Richard might have inherited the chocolate biscuit gene.

The sun was out properly now and the day became a

one-shirt day. We lay on our backs on a patch of mown grass by a farm, the sky a pale blue above us, with puffy white clouds blowing up from the south. I contemplated the map and found that Berwick was now only about six miles away, and the border another four miles after that. Then I closed my eyes and just contemplated.

Ten miles.

I was nearly there.

So had I done what I'd intended all those miles ago? First, there was the challenge. Well, I'd cycled from one end of England to the other. Admittedly with a couple of gaps, but I'd taken such long detours around Herefordshire and Shropshire, that surely I'd been forgiven for the plague-induced interludes. It certainly felt as though I'd completed the challenge. Dorset, Somerset, Wiltshire, Gloucestershire, Herefordshire, Shropshire, Staffordshire, Derbyshire, West Yorkshire, North Yorkshire, County Durham and Northumberland. Far enough.

Then there was really seeing England. I'd definitely done that. I'd cycled through moorland, farmland, hamlets and towns. I'd learned about Gurkhas and their throwing knives, well-dressing in Dorset, and rain in Derbyshire. I'd seen evidence of Romans, Normans and Anglo-Saxons. I'd visited abbeys, cathedrals and castles, and met – figuratively speaking – Richard III and Abraham Darby III, the Percys and the Nevilles, Lord Armstrong and General Vespasian. I'd drunk tea in tea-shops and eaten biscuits almost everywhere else. I'd met friends and made friends – if only long enough to exchange stories and lives.

My brother Andy would say to me later that travelling through England would never be the same again. He's right.

And had I solved the Meaning of Mid-Life? So many of the other travellers I had met were also men in their middle years. Had Mid-Life Crisis hit them? Had they looked in the mirror and seen somebody on the outside who didn't tally with the somebody on the inside? Had their trousers shrunk in the wardrobe?

Or maybe these were people who had just thought, I'd better do this great thing now. Whatever that great thing was. The flashy new car. The new clothes or hairstyle. The cycle ride from one end of the country to the other.

Then again, maybe it was none of those things. Perhaps all the others were fighting-fit men who had always done long-distance bike rides or walks. Or slightly-less-fighting-fit-but-equally-dedicated train spotters or bird watchers. So did that mean that it wasn't a crisis for them at all?

What was it for me then? Had I looked in that mirror? Had my trousers shrunk? ('Yes' to that one, anyway.) And well, that was a nice sports car back in Hamsterley, come to think about it. Little red thing. Mmmm. But not really practical. And where would the kids sit? Where would I put Scott?

This was not good. I had almost finished my journey and I'd not finally resolved one of the last, great mysteries of our time: Mid-Life, the Universe and Everything.

Perhaps I just hadn't cycled far enough to really get to grips with it? Perhaps, when I got to the border, I shouldn't stop, but should head on into Scotland; all in the interests of science, of course. Perhaps -

"Hey, Dad," Richard said. "D'you want a biscuit?"

"Is the Pope a Catholic?"

"What?"

My Irish accent always was hopeless.

"Sorry. I mean yes."

It was time to go home, and, really, I couldn't think of a much better way to do it than this.

"And can you help me with my homework on the way home on the train?"

"Sure. What is it?"

"German."

"Fine."

Germany. Now there's a thought. I probably owed it to mankind.

The sun was still shining as lanes and tracks took us back to the coast and a glorious bit of cycling on a grassy track by the dunes. The path rose slightly and took us above low cliffs looking out to a now-blue sea.

Then Berwick appeared ahead of us. Quite suddenly. The last town in England.

Berwick hasn't always been in England, of course. Until the 13th century, Berwick was one of the greatest of Scots towns. But in 1296 it was unlucky enough to stand in the way of the King who gloried in the name of The Hammer of the Scots. Edward I had indeed hammered at Scotland, reducing it to vassal status, with the sad Scots King in captivity in England. In 1296 Edward was 60 years old, and the Scots were still fighting back. They were to be given a lesson.

For the ordinary people of Berwick the choices must have been stark. To wait behind the town walls and hope that the English went around them. Or to flee with their families and face hunger, cold, and possibly starvation. Some 11,000 are said to have chosen to stay.

On Edward's orders, all were killed. Men, women and children. A piece of history which sounds more like some 20th century events.

Over the two hundred years following Edward I's visit, the town changed hands thirteen times, each time with predictably dire results for the townspeople. The man who finally confirmed Berwick's English status is someone else I'd come across on the route. A certain Richard of Gloucester, the future Richard III.

Our route left the fields and joined town streets, dropping down past houses and businesses into the town. England flags were draped from many of the houses, plus – bravely –

one enormous Scotland flag.

It is a small irony that Berwick Town Football Club plays its games in the Scottish leagues, not the English. An irony that somehow I am glad of.

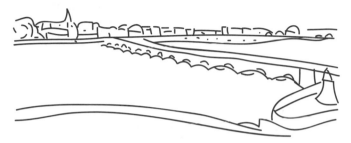

At the wide estuary of the river Tweed, two grand bridges appeared. The first an ancient bridge of stone blocks and small arches stretching maybe a quarter-mile across the water to the town centre on the far side. The second, and the one that the little blue NCN1 signs took us to, was modern and concrete, but with arches that reflected the older bridge next to it. We cycled across and arrived in a wide main street, surprisingly busy for a Sunday morning. It had been part pedestrianised and had a gate in the town wall visible at the top end and the moot hall at the bottom. The town walls were built on the orders of Queen Elizabeth I and still stand almost complete. Berwick is literally surrounded by history. I liked the place, and I was glad that it hadn't been nuked while it was at war with Russia for nigh on a hundred years.

The story goes that after the union of the English and Scottish crowns when Queen Elizabeth I died, Berwick's status was still not settled. For a while, the town had to be specifically named alongside England and Scotland in Acts of Parliament. But when the peace treaty was signed ending the Crimean War against Russia in the 19th century, Berwick was missed out. So Berwick remained at war with Russia.

When in the 1960s a Russian diplomat visited Berwick to

sign a peace treaty, the Mayor commented, "Tell the Russians they can sleep easy in their beds".

Maybe not entirely historically accurate, but excellent stuff.

We bought sandwiches from a baker's and dropped down through a gate in the walls to the river-side walkway to munch them. We sat on the quay, legs dangling over the water.

"Have you enjoyed this, Rich?"

"Yeh, it's been great. Thanks for taking me."

"No. Thanks for coming."

Our legs dangled a while longer, and we took in the wide river and its handsome bridges.

"Last stretch?" I said.

"Yeh."

"Alright Scott?"

"Suppose."

"Rock?"

...

"Rock?"

...

"Doesn't say much, does he, Rock?"

"He is not as other bikes."

"Thank you, Scott. Very philosophical."

"I thought so."

I considered Scott. "Do you realise you've not had a puncture all the way?"

"Yes."

"Nor any sort of mechanically breakdowny thing."

"Yes."

"I think that's rather clever of you."

"So do I."

"Well. Good."

In fact, neither had I. Not a mechanical breakdown, anyway. When my knee had felt odd on hills, I'd slowed.

When my wrist had niggled, I'd rested it. There was just the small matter of the Black Death / Plague that had held me up in Derbyshire. And Wiltshire. Apart from that, I'd been fine.

We cycled back up through the town till we found another of the blue cycle-route signs – the NCN1 was on its way to Edinburgh, and so would take us to the border.

We'd not really been too far that day, but we both felt tired as we moved away from the coast and the hills started.

We were on a B-road, heading up the valley of the Tweed. Four miles to go.

Richard said, "Will there be a sign when we get there?"

"I think so. Surely." We cycled on a bit more. "If we get to Edinburgh, then we're in Scotland."

"Fine."

Even so, I found myself a little nervous as we got closer to where the border must be. It seemed I really needed a sign. Something to show an ending. A completion. I'd done over 1,000 kilometres, over 640 miles, in a great tapestry of a ride – the warp of history and the weft of place. But if I just got to a point where we must be over the border, then turned round and went home, that would feel such an anti-climax. I needed a sign.

Give me a sign, oh Lord.

At the top of a slope, I looked downwards to see – just beyond the dip – a sign. A very big brown sign, with a blue and white thistle:

SCOTLAND
welcomes you

Fantastic.

Brilliant.

I took my feet out of the pedals and free-wheeled down, punching the air.

"Yee-ha!"

Just beyond the sign I braked and looked back. Richard was grinning, ear to ear.

This was just so good. It was wonderful that he was here.

Behind Richard, I spotted another sign. This one was smaller and much, much older. It was originally black writing on a white background, but the black was fading and the white paint was showing rust through. It was overgrown with wild dog-roses in the hedge, whose pink flowers and dark green leaves almost obscured the single word on the sign:

ENGLAND

Captain's log: Day Eighteen
The day's distance: 34.84 miles / 55.74 Km
Average speed: 10.0 mph / 16.0 Kmph
Maximum speed: 28.5 mph / 45.6 Kmph

We set a leisurely pace back into Berwick, straight through the town following signs for the pier and the beach. When we came to a pebbly, sea-weedy patch of beach, I said, "Here we are," and trundled Scott down to the sea.

"Come on, Scott," I said.

"Not again."

"Oh yes."

Captain's log: The Whole Ride
645.79 miles / 1,033.26 Km.
12 counties.
Dorset to Northumberland.
England.

    I wonder how long it would take to cycle from one end of
Germany to the other.
    Perhaps I should mention it to Claire.

Apologies, acknowledgements and thanks

You may have come to the conclusion that I would struggle to recognise a Red Kite from a Red Campion. You are completely right.

However, in my quest for knowledge, I hereby acknowledge the following sources. Without them the accuracy of my work would be highly debatable:

The (1954) *Observer's Book of Birds*. Most recently seen propping up an ancient h-fi unit with a missing leg.

The (1956) *Observer's Book of Wild Flowers*. Now, I couldn't actually find this one, but I would have consulted it if I had, and I'm sure it would have been very good.

A (1964) *History of England*, by Thorn, Lockyer and Smith. Well-thumbed over the years and particularly good for standing on to reach that top shelf.

The (9th century) *Anglo-Saxon Chronicle*, translated in 1953 by Professor GN Garroway, and published in 1972 by JM Dent and Sons

Various English Heritage guide books bought along the way, price £2.99 each.

The internet.

What more could I possibly need?

I have mentioned some excellent books in the text. Their full details are:

The Missing Postman, by Mark Wallington. Published 1993 by Time Warner Paperbacks. (Also a TV series with that man off The Likely Lads, and very good too.)

Neither Here Nor There, by Bill Bryson. Published by all sorts of people, but mine is Black Swan, 1998.

Round Ireland with a Fridge, by Tony Hawks. Published by St Martins Griffin, 2001.

Some names in the text have been changed to protect the innocent, with their voices digitally altered. So if you think you recognise yourself, you don't. It's simply a figment of your fevered imagination.

Thanks are due to Katie Largent for going over my spelling and grammar with a fine toothcomb, to Robin Grenville-Evans for his cover illustration, and to Richard Peace, Dave Freeborn, George East and Jonathon Veale for their help and advice.

Most especially,
thank you so much to my Claire
and to Megan Taylor,
who have encouraged me
to write all this down
and to think that others
might like to read it.

Finally,
this book is particularly dedicated to
Claire, Lisa, Suzie and Richard,
and to my Mum and Dad.

It is also dedicated to those
who have spent good money buying it.
To you I say 'thank you'
and that I sincerely hope
you have found the book

expensive but spotless.

www.bikeridebooks.co.uk